Dear Steve,

   You inspired me to write poems.
   Thank you!

   Shirley Wang Gauf

Sep 2, 2021
   No. 18

Resilience

A First-Generation Chinese-American Woman's
Life Living with Bipolar Disorder

SHIRLEY WANG

Resilience

A First-Generation Chinese-American Woman's Life Living with Bipolar Disorder

©2021 Xiaoling Wang

print ISBN: 978-1-09839-198-0
ebook ISBN: 978-1-09839-199-7

This book is dedicated to my husband Dean and my sons Ryan and Shaun. I would also like to thank my friends and other family members who have been supportive to me.

I would also like to thank Ms. Jessica Saeki for her excellent proofreading and editing work.

Disclaimer: Some names and identifying details have been changed to protect the privacy of individuals.

CHAPTER 1

*H*ere in my palm sits a small Happy Buddha Figurine. It is about one inch tall and wide, a half-inch thick, and made of porcelain. The Happy Buddha has a large belly, which can bear all unbearable things, and a big laugh, laughing at all laughable persons in the world. It was a souvenir brought back by my dad from one of his trips. I received it in my teen years, and it has been with me for over 30 years since. When I moved from China to the U.S., I brought it with me. The Happy Buddha is thought to possess a mighty power, which has protected me over the years.

My grandmother was more or less a Buddhist, like most Chinese people in her time. She was like a mother to me. She raised me until she became paralyzed by a stroke when I was nine years old. She passed away when I was 12.

Six days after I was born, my mother was pronounced dead at a hospital in Shanghai. She got the baby girl she had always wanted during her seven-year marriage to my dad, but she gave her life as the price. After delivery, she developed high blood pressure, due to which a blood vessel in her brain burst. This happened in February of 1968, a chaotic time in China when the whole country was undergoing the Cultural Revolution.

My father was devastated and soon on the edge of a mental breakdown. He was a doctor himself. He worked and lived in Wuhu, a city over 200 miles west of Shanghai on the southern bank of the Yangtze River. My mother worked and lived in Shanghai. My mother and father did not live together, and were only able to visit each other about one month a year with their designated visitation vacation, like many Chinese couples at that time. Traveling by train from Wuhu to Shanghai meant very crowded conditions and took well over ten hours at the time.

I stayed in the hospital nursery for ten days. I developed bad diaper rash. My dad had to work, and he was often sent to work in the countryside far away from home. At that time, if one did not obey those kinds of orders, one could not find work elsewhere and would not be able to survive. My grandmother was 74 years old at that time. It would have been almost impossible for her to take care of me if my dad were to have taken me to Wuhu. Then, my aunt (my father's sister-in-law) in Shanghai said, "Bring the baby into my home, just as if I had another child myself." That is how I was finally brought out of the hospital.

My dad sent 40 yuan out of his 53.5 yuan monthly salary, nearly 75% of his monthly income, to Shanghai in order to support me and grandmother, especially to purchase the expensive imported baby formula to feed me. He lived on the remaining 13.5 yuan, less than 25% of his monthly income, which was very hard for a 35-year-old man. By the end of the month, he would run out of money for food. He would use "liangpiao" to exchange for money on the black market so that he had money to buy food. (At the time, to buy food, one needed liangpiao, which everyone was allotted a certain amount of each month. Liangpiao alone could not buy food, but one could also not buy food without it.)

When I was eight months old, my grandmother and dad brought me to Wuhu. Then, when I was 13 months old, my dad had to be away from home again, so my other aunt in Shanghai let us stay at her home. This aunt was my dad's older sister and lived in a very small apartment with her daughter's family. When I arrived, there were three babies in the household (the other two being my aunt's two grandsons, born the same year as I was).

When I was 18 months old, my grandmother took me back to Wuhu to be with my dad. We settled in Wuhu and lived there from that point on.

CHAPTER 2

*M*y father, grandmother, and I lived in a room on the first floor of a two-story dormitory building, built with red bricks, at the medical college where my father taught as a lecturer. This one room was our bedroom, dining room, kitchen, and bathroom. We had no modern toilets - only "piss pots." It was our home.

During the day, my father went to work; only my grandmother and I were at home. My father still had to go on out-of-town trips for week-long stretches. At one time, the only occupants of the entire building, even the whole college campus, were my 70-something-year-old grandmother and I, a young toddler.

When my grandmother was cooking on the coal stove or doing other chores, she would turn a rectangular stool upside down and put me inside, as if putting me in a playpen. I could not move, but it at least kept me safe, especially from the burning stove.

One evening at dinner time, grandmother brought a clay pot full of sizzling pork stew to our little round table. It was hot off the stove. The pork stew was my father's favorite dish. My grandmother was a great cook. In those days, food was scarce, and each person could only buy about a pound of meat in a month. All of a sudden, I slipped off my chair and fell under the table, and down with me went the pot of hot stew. My father and grandmother were startled, fearing that I would get burned. They rushed to pick me up. Luckily, I was all right, not hurt at all. I cried out of fear. It was a great pity that the pot of meat went to waste.

Grandmother seemed to have endless chores to do. We had no TV, not even a radio. My long days were filled with lonesomeness and boredom. My entire living space was that one room. At one end was a door that seemed to be closed all the time; at the other end was a window. Outside of the window was the brushy slope of Iron Hill. I used to squat behind my small bamboo chair, and from that angle I could see the sky, broken up by tree branches. I used to stare at the broken sky through the window for hours at a time. That was my world.

I would wait and wait until finally evening fell and my dad came home. The best time of my day then began. My dad would pick me up, throw me over his head, sit me on his lap, and sing Chinese nursery rhymes with me in Shanghai dialect: "Bing bing, bang bang! Hey, someone is knocking at the door! Who's there? It's me. Who are you? I am…" or "Sitting line by line, sharing apples, dad comes home to pinch our earlobes."

My dad also made origami grasshoppers, balls, and cranes for me. Our home was filled with laughter, my own giggles and squeals. If only my dad had not had to go on those week-long trips from time to time…

I remember one evening when my dad let me sit on his shoulders. He took me for a walk along the railway tracks near the college. We were walking toward the rich orange sunset. The sun was so big, like a giant egg yolk hanging low in the sky. I will cherish that simple moment with my dad forever.

One night, my dad took me to watch outdoor movies at the college sports field. There were not many movies at that time for us to see. This one was an anti-Japanese war movie. It looked very scary to me. When one Japanese soldier wielded his katana sword over his head, I couldn't help but cry. My dad hurriedly took me home.

When I was a little older, my grandmother took me to visit the neighbors who also lived in the same building. I remember visiting Grandma Wang, Uncle "Fat" and his wife, and Aunt Meng and her husband, Uncle Chu. On the second floor lived Grandpa An. One day, he had some unusual visitors - some monkeys, possibly from Mount Zhe where there was a zoo. Those monkeys opened his cookie jar and stole his cookies.

On one of my visits to Uncle "Fat," he and his wife tried to get me to say hello to them. I was usually a sweet, open child and greeted people whenever I saw them, but for some reason, I refused to do so that day. His wife put some nuts into one of my little hands. To everyone's surprise, I threw them on the ground. My grandmother took me home right away and told my dad. The two people who loved me most punished me by beating my palm. While I was sobbing, my dad asked me to promise to never behave like that again. Then they brought me to Uncle "Fat's" house to give my apologies. I was just around three years old.

One day, one of my dad's medical school classmates, Aunt Yang, brought her daughter Min to visit us. Min was a couple of years older than I. The two of us played with wooden blocks and had great fun. Min had a little bucket made of tin. Later on, I learned that Min's father, also a doctor, was shot in the head and killed by the rebel faction in the heat of "Wu Dou" (militant fighting between two factions, the royalists and the rebels, during the Cultural Revolution). He had been completely innocent, with no involvement whatsoever with either faction. He was shot only because he mistakenly answered when the rebels were actually calling the name of someone else which sounded similar to his own. He was in his mid-30s, leaving behind his wife and young daughter.

Aunt Meng felt my dad's life was difficult without a woman. She introduced her colleague Ms. Zhou to him. Ms. Zhou was in her late 30s, divorced with no children, about four years older than my dad and not particularly good-looking. My dad was a very handsome man and a very good doctor. Zhou soon fell in love with my dad. My dad hesitated, but he had to find someone to marry because rumors were circulating that he would have to be away from home for longer spells.

Ms. Zhou became my step-mother when I was around three years old. I still remember the day they got married. I heard people were talking about "chi xi jiu" ("to eat a happy meal," referring to wedding banquets). My grandmother and I stayed at home and did not attend the wedding banquets.

After they got married, my father and step-mother were given a separate room behind the bathroom of the building. It was very dark and noisy, but they were very happy to have their own space.

In the beginning, my step-mother was nice to me. I was very happy to be able to call someone "Ma Ma" ("mother" in Chinese).

My step-mother did not spend much time with us, since she was working in the countryside at that time. When I was a little over four years old, she took me to the countryside where she worked. She was pregnant. I loved that village. I made friends with a local girl named Xia who was a couple of years older than I. She would carry her younger brother on her back, and together we would rock him in his crib. One day, the crib turned over, but luckily Xia's little brother was unhurt. I got to walk barefoot along the ridges of rice patties and stand in a small creek, watching little fish swimming by my legs.

CHAPTER 3

$\mathcal{S}$hortly after we came back from the countryside, my step-mother's water broke. It was still too early for the baby to be born, so my step-mother was hospitalized and ordered to stay in bed to delay the onset of labor. During that time, I went to stay at my uncle's home (my step-mother's younger brother). They lived in an alley in downtown Wuhu. They had three rooms and an attic, which was my favorite hideout. I played with my three step-cousins who were a lot older than I. They were all very good to me. I especially liked my cousin Dong who was very funny, making me laugh all the time.

When I was brought to the maternity hospital to see my step-mother, I noticed her belly was huge. She let me listen to the baby's heartbeat by placing my ear to a special cone-shaped stethoscope. Of course, I could not hear a thing. The adults teased me, asking me to guess the gender of the baby. I said it was a boy.

Soon my step-mother went into labor. She used all her strength, but she could not push the baby's head out. The doctors used a suction device to aid the delivery, bringing into the world a baby girl. At the age of 42, my step-mother had her first and only child. Everybody was thrilled.

When I got to see my half-sister in the nursery, she looked ugly to me. She was so tiny, with wrinkled yellowish-red skin and an elongated head with dark hair. Nevertheless, I was excited, not yet knowing that the birth of this little girl would change my life forever.

By the time the baby and my step-mother were discharged from the hospital, we moved from the medical college at Iron Hill to Yijishan Hospital by the Yangtze River. Both my dad and step-mother worked at this hospital. My step-mother was a nurse-turned-gynecologist. The hospital had been established in 1887 by a group of American Christian missionaries. It was located on a small hill by the Yangtze River. At one time, many famous doctors had worked at this hospital. It was one of the best in Southern Anhui. It was closed during the peak of the Cultural Revolution but ordered to reopen in the middle of 1972.

Our home was a one-story house shaped like a U. My grandmother and I lived in a big room in the middle section. This room was divided into the family room and our bedroom with a partition. My grandmother and I shared the same bed. She used to tell me stories and pamper me with snacks she bought with her pocket money.

She liked to read books in bed with her magnifier. She never went to a formal school, like most Chinese women in her time. She learned how to read from a teacher her parents hired to teach her at home. She did not learn how to write, though. She could only write her name in Chinese characters. My grandmother's feet were bound when she was a small girl, following the tradition of that time. It was so painful that she cried. Her parents gave in and set her feet free eventually. As a result, her feet were bigger than those of other old women with small feet, but still deformed.

My grandmother was the youngest and only daughter of her parents, who had owned and run an old store selling stationary goods (writing paper, pen brushes, ink, and so on) in old Shanghai. She was born in 1894. She had two older brothers who had studied in France, learning nothing yet spending the family's fortune.

When she was young, my grandmother was very good-looking. Her parents loved her very much, and they were very picky about who she should marry. They did not want her to marry someone who was too rich to love her and treat her well, nor someone who was too poor to offer her a decent life. As a result, my grandmother did not marry until age 26, a very old age to get married at a time when most girls were married around the age of 18.

My grandfather was four years older than my grandmother and died four years before I was born. I was told that he was born in Tianjin (a big port city right next to Beijing) to a Muslim family. At the age of 16, his mother said to him, "Son, you have come of age. Go to your older brother and ask him to let you serve as a soldier under him." His older brother was a general of the Qing Dynasty based in the Fujian area. My grandfather went there and, upon hearing his words, his older brother told him, "Take this money as your travel fee and go back home. If you want to be a soldier, you can be one anywhere but under me." His older brother was not corrupt and wanted to avoid nepotism.

My grandfather was stubborn. He thought it would be shameful to go home. He went to Shanghai, enrolled in a police academy, and became a police officer. He even went to Japan to study for a year. Japan was a popular destination for young people in China to study new ideas at that time. As a police officer, my grandfather used to take his men to exercise at the old drill ground in the heart of old Shanghai. On his way, he would pass my great-grandparents' store, where my grandmother sat in her upstairs room by the window doing needlework. He saw her and fell in love. Sometimes he would pretend to be shopping in order to get a closer look at her when she was helping out at the store.

Shortly after, my grandfather sent his best friend, "Drum Zhang," who headed the marching band of the police team, to be the matchmaker to talk to my great grandparents. At that time, marriages were arranged by a couple's parents.

My great-grandparents said to Drum Zhang, "We are merchants, and you are men of the ranks. We are like the water in the well, which doesn't mix with water in the river."

Zhang came back with this message to my great grandparents: "If you don't agree to this marriage, you will prepare to pack and leave." (In China at that time, the police could harass the people.)

My great-grandparents then proposed some conditions: "First, our daughter will not be a concubine; and if you have ever been married before, you must get a divorce."

My grandfather said, "Deal."

The second and third clauses were that my grandmother would live in Shanghai and never go live with her mother-in-law in Tianjin, and that the children would not adopt my grandfather's religion, which was Islam. My grandfather answered both with one word: "Deal."

My grandfather kept his word, divorced his first wife from an arranged marriage whom he never loved, and married my grandmother. They had five children; my father was their youngest. My grandmother lost two of her sons in their early twenties to tuberculosis. She was devastated. This is why my father wanted to become a doctor.

After the Japanese attacked Shanghai in August 1937, my grandfather moved to Chongqing in Sichuan to be with the government in exile. After a fierce fight, Shanghai fell into the hands of the Japanese in November of that year. My grandmother took her five children (my dad being only four years old at that time) to take the train to Nanjing to board the ships going to Chongqing along the Yangtze River. When the train traveled just outside of Nanjing, news arrived that Nanjing had fallen and that Japanese soldiers were massacring the Chinese people there. The train chugged back to Shanghai.

The family got separated during the war. Later, my grandfather cheated on my grandmother and had children with a nurse he met at a Chongqing hospital. The money he had been sending back to Shanghai became unreliable. My grandmother had a hard time running the family. She did not learn about my grandfather's affair until much later, when my grandfather came to visit family in Shanghai and a letter from that nurse with a picture of her and her baby fell into the hands of my grandmother by chance. My grandmother was so angry that she decided she would not live under the same roof with my grandfather ever again, although they never officially divorced.

My grandmother was loved by all her grandchildren. She was very loving herself. She was like an old hen who protected and loved me. Because of her, my early childhood was a happy one which shielded me against the hardships that were to follow.

CHAPTER 4

To our left side lived the Li family. At the end of the left section was my step-mother and dad's room, and my baby sister lived with them there. To our right lived the Zhu family. Both the Li and Zhu families had a girl my age, and we went to elementary school together.

We did not have air conditioning then. Summers in Wuhu were hot. I miss those summer nights when we all brought our bamboo summer beds or folding chairs out to the open ground outside our homes. We would lie on them, waving our fans made of palm leaves to cool off. We would stare up at the star-studded night sky. There was no pollution then, and the stars were many and bright. We listened to the adults tell stories, such as the "the Cowherd and the Weaving Maid", in which one of the Mother of Heaven's weaving maids, an immortal girl from the celestial heaven, fell in love with a mortal cowherd and married him in secret. Later on, the Mother of Heaven found out and became furious. She took the maid back to heaven, while the cowherd flew behind, wearing his magic cow's hides. Just as he was about to catch up to them, the Mother of Heaven struck out with her hair pin and created the Silver River (the Milky Way) to separate the couple, and they became stars. All the birds on earth were sympathetic of their fate and volunteered to fly there to form a bridge, allowing them to meet once a year on the seventh day of the seventh month of the lunar calendar. This was one of my favorite stories. I tried to find the lovers from the story and the Milky Way on those midsummer nights.

We also listened to the adults talk about things like the lavish dinner with which Premier Zhou Enlai entertained U.S. president Richard Nixon in early 1970s on his historic visit to China. According to rumor, one dish was made with thin threads of Chinese ham stuffed through the stems of bean sprouts. How much labor and skill it must have taken to make that dish!

There was a pond near the house we lived in. The pond was covered with duckweeds in the summer. Those duckweeds were as green as emeralds. I saw people scooping them up with fishing nets. They would bring the duckweeds home to feed their ducks.

The hospital built a pig pen by the pond to raise pigs for meat to serve at the staff cafeteria. I watched the pigs grow from piglets into adult pigs weighing a couple hundred pounds. Then came the exciting time to slaughter them. The hospital hired some butchers to slaughter the pigs on the open ground right outside of the hospital cafeteria, which was not far from the house where we lived. It always attracted a lot of onlookers, especially us kids. The sharp screech of the pigs pleading for their lives still lingers in my ears even to this day. The butchers would slash a pig's throat and let out all the blood. Then they would poke a hole with a long iron stick underneath the pig's skin from one of its hind legs. One of the men would blow air through the hole, pumping up the pig's body into a ball. This way, it became easier to shave the hair off the pig's skin. After shaving came the most interesting part: opening up the pig's belly to take out the organs. It sounds gross, but it was great fun for us kids at a time when there was little entertainment.

After that, we could buy meatballs from the hospital cafeteria. They were very soft and tasted delicious. I still miss them to this day. There were a few great cooks at the cafeteria. They made excellent "bao zi" (meat or vegetable stuffed buns).

My father gave my grandmother a small battery-powered transistor radio. It brought some entertainment to our lives. In the beginning, most of the programs were the eight Beijing Operas composed under Madame Mao (Chairman Mao's wife). Later, there were more programs. We even heard pieces of classical music from time to time. Those music notes felt like cool water from a spring touching my heart. I was often moved to tears.

We had some children's books. Children's books at that time were like comic strips. They were about three by four inches in size, and about a half-inch thick. On each page was one big picture, usually hand-drawn by real artists in black and white.

Underneath the pictures were a few lines of words in Chinese telling the story illustrated by the pictures. Some of the books' pictures were screenshots of popular movies of that time, usually in black and white. Some of the books were political propaganda. I remember reading one book telling the story of a Soviet child whose birthday present of a dress shrank to the size of doll clothes after one wash. Another book was about an American boy who went to the zoo only to see his own father dressed up in a gorilla costume playing the part of a gorilla. Those books tried to show us what happy lives we were living compared to miserable lives of people in Soviet Russia or capitalist America. Later on, we had some better books. Among them, the historic stories, especially the four classics, (Dream of the Red Chamber, Outlaws of the Marsh, The Romance of Three Kingdoms and Journey to the West) were my all-time favorites. These books have become pricey collectibles nowadays.

Later on, we added an addition onto the room my grandmother and I shared. It became our kitchen. About 100 feet outside of the kitchen door, there was a huge, old elm tree. Every year its seeds would fall and cover the ground. One season, there was a strong typhoon which brought down that old elm. It barely missed hitting our kitchen. Its branches blocked the entrance to the kitchen from outside.

After my step-mother gave birth to my sister, she became distant to me. One morning, my father angrily brought me to the room he, my step-mother, and my baby sister shared. My step-mother was lying in bed, frowning. It turned out that she was very upset after having heard from others that I had said she was not my real mother. I had, in fact, heard that said by other adults and then told other people I knew, and the words had reached my step-mother's ears. My father pointed to my step-mother and said to me, "Look, who is she?" "She is mama (mother)." I responded sheepishly. Then my dad said, again solemnly, "Remember, daughter, this IS your mama." After that, my step-mother started to be mean to me.

Around the age of six, she made me do chores like washing dishes under the water faucet about 50 feet away from the house, which we shared with the neighbors. I often dropped porcelain bowls or spoons on the cement ground and broke them. I was blamed for these accidents. When my father was not at home, she verbally abused me by accusing me of being lazy. She used to tell me the story of a lazy kid who died because he was too lazy to turn over the big pancake his mother put around his neck before she went on a trip. I did have a lot of imperfections; I was a slow eater, I was not very good at doing chores like sweeping the floors, and I would put my dirty handkerchiefs in a drawer and wash them only when the drawer was full. When my shoes became too small, she kept putting off buying me bigger shoes, saying instead that my feet grew too fast. She said that my feet needed to be contained so that they would not grow too big, so that I would not turn into a big-footed woman whom it would be hard to find a husband for. So, I walked around in those small shoes, walking on my curled-up toes. It was very painful.

Nevertheless, I liked my little half-sister. My step-mother had plenty of milk, and my baby sister's cheeks soon grew plump. She was so cute. I carried her on my back, like my friend from the countryside, Xia, used to do to her little brother. When she was about two years old, our neighbor Uncle Zhu gave her a crew-cut, making her look just like a little boy. She was athletic, the very opposite of me. We played together. I made a "house" using chairs and umbrellas, and she loved it. Later on, the pond was filled with dirt, and the hospital began building a four-story dormitory for interns from the medical college about 100 feet from our house. There were sand piles near the construction site not far from our kitchen door. My sister and I played in the sand all day during the summer. We dug holes, covered them up with twigs and old newspaper, and then put sand on top. We would then lure other kids to walk on them, laughing when they fell. When it was bath-time, my dad would have us stand in a small wood basin and pour several bucketfuls of water on top of our heads. The basin would soon be covered with a thick layer of sand. My sister and I would then take our bath in a big wood bath basin. We had lots of simple fun.

We also got very lucky that my dad escaped drowning on a sinking ferry boat. He was sent on a trip to the countryside. He went with a few of his colleagues. They had to cross a big river by ferry boat. It was raining. My dad and his colleagues decided to stay overnight and cross the river the next day. Shortly after they made that decision, the ferry boat collided with a big ship, capsized, and sank to the bottom of the river. Many people died. My father and his colleagues narrowly escaped.

CHAPTER 5

*S*oon, I started elementary school. At age six, I went to first grade, even though the minimum age for first grade was actually seven at that time. I did okay in school. I remember that one of my classmates named Gang drowned playing along the Yangtze River. The two other kids who had gone with him were too frightened to ask for help from the adults until it was too late. Gang's mother was so sad that she cried, "Oh good heaven, if you were to take one of my sons, why didn't you pick my second son, who is an idiot?" I could not imagine what the little boy who lost his brother must have thought, being cursed like that by his own mother.

The next year, I could not advance to second grade because someone found out that I was a year younger and made me stay in first grade for another year. This turned out to be not a bad idea, as I was now older and excelled at school. The teachers were good to me, and I liked school. It was a place to escape from the accusations of my step-mother.

The school was right next to home, separated by a wall. However, to get to school, we had to walk out of the hospital and around the building for a little over ten minutes. We walked to school on our own without the company of adults. Sometimes, a few older kids acted like bullies, trying to stop us. I was scared and had to run once in a while. The way to school was not always smooth when we were young.

Most windows at the school had their glass panels missing. The teachers asked us kids whose parents worked at the hospital to bring used X-ray sheets to patch up the windows. I remember scrubbing the dark film off the X-ray sheets so that they would be brighter. In winter, the classrooms were so cold that we used to bring charcoal to school to warm us up, especially during exams. Every classroom had a portrait of Chairman Mao hanging above the blackboard. On each side was written his quotation "Hao hao xue xi, tian tian xiang shang," which means "study hard, make daily progress" (or more literally, "good good study, day day up"). We had to take turns cleaning the classrooms and even the filthy restroom shared by the entire school on the other end of the sports ground.

In 1976, the hospital decided to build apartment buildings on the site of the house we lived in, to accommodate the growing number of staff and their families. Our neighbors, the Li and Zhu families, and my family were all moved to another location. We lived on the ground level of a two-story building. Above us were rooms to be used to treat patients using isotope therapy. We were there temporarily and would move back into the new apartments once they became ready. We brought Grandmother's cat with us. I loved that cat.

In the summer of 1976, Tangshan, a mining city not far from Beijing, had a big earthquake (magnitude 7.8), which killed over 240,000 people and severely wounded more than another 160,000. The whole country was in shock. The hospital sent teams of doctors and nurses to help and later on treated some of the wounded, even though we were over 600 miles south. With little knowledge of earthquakes, fear was circulating. People feared that earthquakes would strike their cities. People in Wuhu were no exception. The adults in the hospitals built tents in open areas, and we would spend some of our nights out in those tents to escape the danger of the earthquakes. It was fun for us kids.

One morning in early September, September 9th, 1976, we were told that there would be a very important announcement later that day and that we should be prepared. Not knowing what it could possibly be, people thought it might be about an earthquake coming. Grandmother prepared food in case of an emergency and took me and my sister to the tent we shared with our neighbors. Later, the loudspeaker played funeral music, and a sad voice announced the passing of Chairman Mao. The impact was much bigger than the earthquake that had disrupted the lives of the people all over China. It was as if the sky had fallen. Sad funeral music loomed over the whole country. According to Chinese tradition, memorials called "ling tang" (soul houses) were set up all over the place, including the hospital and our school. Everyone wore black armbands and white flowers to mourn Chairman Mao. We made those white flowers with thin, white tissue paper. On the day our school held our official morning ceremony, everybody appeared to be crying. Some people were crying so sadly that they seemed to pass out. I was eight years old and could not make myself cry like the others. I feared that I would get into trouble if I did not. I faked it, burying my head in my arms. That year was a sad year for China with many deaths, beginning with the passing of beloved premier Zhou Enlai.

Shortly after Mao's death, his wife and her comrades, the "Gang of the Four," were ousted. This marked the end of the Cultural Revolution. The whole country switched into a big celebratory mood. Actors acted out comical plays by dressing up like the "Gang of the Four," who were made into clowns. Even some of my classmates copied such plays and made us laugh. Not long ago, those four were so powerful that they were untouchable. What a dramatic change! Rumors went around saying that everything Madame Mao had was fake: she had fake hair, teeth, breasts, and buttocks. Deng Xiao Ping came into power, ushering in reform and unprecedented economic growth.

My early years at school were easy. There was not much homework. We had lots of fun. My best friends were Jie and Ying. Jie's mother, Aunt Shen, was one of my step-mother's best friends. The three of us hung out together a lot. Aunt Shen was not Jie's biological mother. She had never married and had adopted Jie from one of her brothers. Jie's home always had lots of cool toys. I remember she had a tin piggy bank with a little lock which could be opened by a key. Aunt Shen even had an organ in her home. She tried to teach me how to play the organ, but I could not coordinate my hands. She also taught me many songs. Educated in missionary schools where she learned her English, Aunt Shen taught English classes to us neighborhood kids one summer. That's where I learned my first English words: "book," "school," "boy," "girl," etc. We used to mimic the sounds of English with Chinese words. She was very funny and spoke with a Nanjing dialect accent. She taught us quips like, "English words, you don't need to know many; yes and no are all you need to know, if any." She ignited my interest in English, which changed my life later on. I started to learn English at school around age nine or ten, and my first lesson was "Long live Chairman Mao."

Jie had relatives living in the United States. In the late 1970s, Aunt Shen brought home a small nine-inch black-and-white TV one day. It was the first TV any people in the entire hospital had ever seen. Aunt Shen let people come to her home (which was one big room) to watch TV. Every night, that room was packed with people, staring at the tiny screen. During the summer, she would put the TV outside so that more people could watch it. I was one of those who frequented her home for the TV. I remember watching one Japanese movie called "The Story of the Fox" and the American TV series "Man from Atlantis." We loved those shows.

I often played by the side of the Yangtze river in the summer. I would watch the ships and barges going up and down the Yangtze at sunset. I also sat on the rocks to watch fisherman catching fish with their big nets for hours. I love seeing those fish jumping in the nets. Those images were engraved in my memories.

CHAPTER 6

*A*fter Deng Xiaoping came into power, work at my elementary school became more serious. The government wanted to bring "the Four Modernizations" (referring to industrial, agricultural, national defense, science and technological advancements) to China. In order to achieve this goal, great emphasis was put on education. I entered 4th grade at that time - not too late to catch up with my studies. I started to work hard. I stayed up late into the night to study every day.

At that time, education resources were scarce. China adopted a system of "key" middle and high schools. In each city there were a few middle or high schools designated as key schools ("zhong dian zhong xue"). Kids would take an exam to determine if they could be accepted into these key schools. Those who went to key schools would have a better chance of passing the rigorous college entrance exam to gain entry into colleges or universities, leading to a much better career later on. It was not fair, but China had limited resources at that time. Colleges and universities reopened after the disruption of the Cultural Revolution, and the country restarted issuing annual, nation-wide college entrance examinations in 1977. Only a small proportion of students who took the exam could pass and gain entry into colleges or universities. Competition was intense.

I spent 5th grade studying hard. At the end of 5th grade, I took the exam and got a good score, and I was accepted into Middle School Affiliated with Anhui Normal University, one of the only three key middle and high schools in Wuhu. Wuhu had a population of around half a million people at that time, and only a handful of the kids at my elementary school were accepted into any of those key middle schools.

While I was busy studying, my beloved grandmother suffered a stroke which left her paralyzed and bedridden. My father hired a caregiver to take care of her, but while my parents went to work and us kids to school, my grandmother didn't receive good care. Three years after her stroke, my grandmother passed away at the age of 86, when I was 12.

While we were living in the transitional building waiting for the staff apartment to be built, my step-mother often humiliated me in front of my friends in the neighborhood. She rarely bought me clothes. I wore old-fashioned pants hand-made by my grandmother before she had her stroke. Those pants did not fit me well. My step-mother joked in front of my friends that my pants were so baggy that I could go steal a chicken and hide it inside my pants. Being at a delicate age of self-consciousness, I felt very humiliated.

After waiting for about two years, the staff apartment building was completed, and my father got an apartment on the second floor. This was the first time for us to live in an apartment that had a separate kitchen with a sink, and a bathroom with a squat pan that we could flush with running water. After we moved to the new apartment, my step-mother did not bring my grandmother's cat with us. It became a feral cat. I was very sad, but I could not do anything about it. I felt so powerless.

Our long-time neighbors, the Li and Zhu families, also moved into that new apartment building, but in separate units. We no longer saw them every day. We had more privacy, but we lost the daily interactions and closeness of our old neighborhood.

My father worked very hard. He was an ear, nose, and throat doctor. Sometimes there were emergency cases to which he was called on in the middle of the night. He saved many lives. He also spent his nights writing educational books on how to take care of the health of our ears, noses, and throats. He published four of those books, and he also published many articles in national medical journals. In China, patients tend to give gifts to their doctors out of gratitude, but my father never accepted those. Sometimes, a patient would find where we lived and come to our apartment to give those gifts to my father, yet still he always refused. China also started to treat intellectuals better during that time. My father became the head of the department he worked in. He also became a professor at the medical college.

My father always encouraged me to work hard. He subscribed to children's science and literature magazines to enrich my learning. I liked to read. In reading, I could escape from my step-mother's harsh words and find a world of wonder.

We also bought our own black-and-white TV. However, I now had to study and did not watch it as much as I had watched the little 9-inch TV at Aunt Shen's house.

China also started to enforce its "one-child" policy. A couple was only allowed to have one child, in order to curtail the large and growing population. My step-mother was assigned a job to work in the family planning office at the hospital. She was not very happy about this, because she missed some opportunities to be promoted to a higher rank. Her relationship with my father was not a good one. My father was very dedicated and proud of his work. However, my step-mother did not want him to work so hard. They disagreed on many things. They came from very different backgrounds. My step-mother was very frugal. She always tried to save money. She rarely approved my father's plans to buy something. As their relationship deteriorated, my step-mother blamed me more. After seeing her treating me badly, my father got upset. It became a vicious cycle.

However, outside of our home, my step-mother was perceived to be a very nice person. She was nice to other people. A lady who worked at a grocery supply agency, who also used to be one of my step-mother's patients, befriended her. During that time, China was still under the influence of the planned economy, leaving a shortage of supplies. We were still on a ration system. To purchase meat, oil, sugar, and almost all other necessities still required a special government-issued ticket or coupon. Because of her access to these precious goods through her work, this lady helped my step-mother to buy eggs, nicer cuts of meat, and so on. In return, my step-mother would introduce her to doctors she needed to see. This friend of my step-mother's helped us gain access to better food during that time of scarcity. This helped greatly in providing better nutrition to my growing body.

CHAPTER 7

$\mathcal{S}$oon, I started middle school. My middle school was located in the heart of Wuhu, about a 30-minute walk from home, not far from the medical college. The walk was along several major streets. Kids from the hospital who went to the same middle school usually took the shuttle bus used by staff who commuted between the hospital and medical college, which were affiliated, as nobody had personal cars at that time. I often missed the bus and had to walk to school.

The school was divided into two campuses by a street. One campus was the middle school, and the other campus was the high school. The middle school campus was very beautiful. It sat on a hill. The main building was a three-story red brick building surrounded by pathways covered by tree arches. When I was on breaks, I liked to walk under those tree arches along the pathways, but later the school cut down those trees due to concerns it blocked light to the classrooms. I felt very sad to lose those beautiful tree arches.

There were about 50 students in each class. Each grade had six classes. Boys played with boys, girls with girls, and boys and girls did not talk to each other. There were three dominant girls in my class who always hung out together. At one time, I offended one of them somehow, and then the gang turned against me. They isolated me. Whenever they saw any other girls playing with me, they would drag those girls away from me. They bullied me. It lasted for almost a year. I was miserable. It finally came to an end after one kind girl in the class acted as a go-between to help me make up with them.

On the other hand, I did well academically. I was not very good at math, but I was good at other subjects. I had some very good teachers at the middle school. My English teacher was a petite lady with a strong Fujianese accent, a Filipino-Chinese woman who returned to China in the 1950s. She was a gymnast when she was young, and she was very elegant. She was the lead teacher of our class. She was very humorous, and she was very nice to me. I also liked our physics teacher, who was very good at explaining concepts in physics. He also had a great sense of humor. We did not get to take many art or music lessons, because the school put more emphasis on academic lessons. Very few of my fellow students had the luxury of learning to play a musical instrument.

Since school was far away from home, we ate lunch at the school. We brought our aluminum lunch boxes to school, and the school cafeteria would steam them. We then ate our lunches during lunch breaks. The mother of one of my friends had some friends at a nearby shoe factory which had a nice cafeteria. My friend and I ate lunches at that shoe factory cafeteria for a while. One day after lunch, an older boy from the school who also ate lunch at the shoe factory followed me on my way back to school. Once I arrived at the school and passed a popsicle vendor, the boy bought me a popsicle. I was so scared, I ran away as fast as I could. I was a seventh grader at that time. Contact with boys was taboo.

Three years of middle school soon passed. Again I did well on the high school entrance exam and got to go to the high school campus of this key middle school.

The high school was located on the other side of the road. There were about 60 students in a class. Each grade had four classes. I made many lifelong friends there. Boys and girls still did not talk to each other. With surging hormones, I started to feel attracted to the boys, but I dared not to fall in love. That was still a taboo. During my high school years, Taiwan and Hong Kong pop songs became popular among the students. We had some boys and girls who were very good at singing those songs, and they would do so when we held our New Year parties. Some of them were very talented. We also watched Japanese soap operas on TV at home. Among the boys, wuxia (kung fu) novels written by famous Hong Kongese author Louis Cha Leung-yung, better known under the pen name Jin Yong (Gum Yoong in Cantonese) were extremely popular. I didn't read them myself - I read books by Taiwanese romance novelist Qiong Yao (Chiung Yao as spelled in Taiwan), like many girls did at that time. I spent hours at a stretch reading those novels and shed some tears for those characters. During those years, the Chinese women's volleyball team did very well and became the world champions, which inspired a strong love of volleyball among us students. We played or watched volleyball matches after school. I also played volleyball with friends, although I was not good enough to play in actual matches.

After the first year of high school, we had to choose between paths of liberal arts or science and engineering. At the time, the liberal arts path offered fewer career opportunities compared to the science and engineering path. I also did not want to leave my classmates to go to a newly-formed liberal arts path class. I decided to choose the science and engineering path and remained in my class with most of my classmates. At that time, there was a saying circulating around: "Those who master Math, Physics and Chemistry will prevail."

We all had to take political science lessons, and it was one subject tested in the college entrance exams. We had to learn Marxist economic theory. The teacher kept telling us in the class that Capitalism was rotten to the core and that it was dying, although it would take a long, long time. I didn't like this subject, but the teacher was good. He made the lessons more tolerable. In writing, we had to write argumentative assays, which I was not good at. We were given topics such as "flared trousers and beauty" to write an essay about. At that time, flared pants were popular. The teacher wanted us to write about the need to focus on inner beauty rather than appearances, but I just couldn't come up with any such arguments. I was less focused on my studies in my high school years, probably due to surging hormones in youthful body.

My life at home during middle school and high school were miserable due to my step-mother's constant verbal abuse. She seldom abused me physically, but her harsh words hit me hard. I often cried in my room for hours. I thought about committing suicide by drinking insecticide. I did not dare to do it, but I thought about it many times. She accused me of being lazy and called me a hooker. She said all kinds of unthinkable words. One time, she cursed at me and beat me with a stick in front of one of my good friends. Another time, she tore up the newspaper I was reading in front of a family friend.

Once during my high school years, she had an argument with my father. She kicked open the door to my room and beat me with her fists. She got so angry that she took a kitchen knife and waved it in front of me, threatening that she would kill me first and then my father. My father finally had had enough and wanted a divorce. After seeing my father was serious, she regretted her outburst. She started to cook some nice food and be kind to me, asking me to bring my father to eat the meal she had cooked. At that time in China, divorce was considered shameful. I also thought about my sister; I did not want her to lose her father. I asked my father to not go through with a divorce. After that, my step-mother did not do such extreme things, but the verbal abuse still persisted.

Finally, it was the time for the most important exam in my life: the college entrance exam. It lasted three days. When the results came out, I learned that I passed, and even passed the higher threshold for entering key colleges/universities, although not by very much. Around half of the graduates from my high school passed the exam and could go to colleges or universities. We had to submit a list of colleges/universities we wanted to go to and majors we wanted to study. I decided to study medicine, which students on the science and engineering path could choose. I also wanted to leave Wuhu, a relatively small city, and go to Shanghai, the most advanced cosmopolitan city in China. I chose Shanghai Medical University, the alma mater of my father. It was among the top two medical universities in China at that time. It required a high score to get in. My score was not high enough for me to major in medicine there, even though it would have easily allowed me to be accepted to the medical college in Wuhu (where my father worked. I could have majored in medicine and become a doctor if I chose the medical college in Wuhu.). I read in a Shanghai Medical University flyer that they had a new major of nursing. It was the second year the university had offered a four-year nursing major with a bachelor's degree. (Previously, nurses in China only went through three years of training after finishing middle school.) I chose this new major at Shanghai Medical University hoping to become a leader in the field of nursing in China one day.

That summer, my father sent me to Nanjing to visit my mother's younger sister's family. I had never met my aunt and her family before. After I was born and my mother died, my father had some disputes with my maternal grandparents. As a result, I never got to see them. My aunt and uncle were very nice people. I tried to learn as much as I could about my mother, even though I could not get much information from them. I learned that my mother was a nutrition nurse at a hospital in Shanghai specializing in treating patients with tuberculosis. My uncle was a pathology professor at Nanjing Medical University. My aunt had two children close to my age. We got along well. I had a good time at my aunt's. Soon, I was going to start a brand-new chapter in my life.

CHAPTER 8

*W*hen it was time to go to Shanghai for college, my father left for Yemen as a member of a team of doctors from Anhui province to provide medical aid to the people there. China had been sending doctors and other aid workers to Arab and African countries at that time. Those were good assignments for the doctors, because they could earn U.S. dollars and buy things that were luxury goods in China at the time, like color TVs, refrigerators, washing machines, and high-end stereo systems. My father would be gone for two years. I took the crowded train with my friends and went to Shanghai to start my college life.

My cousin in Shanghai met me at the train station and later took me to my university. The university was located in downtown Shanghai. We went to my dorm. It was located on the first floor of a five-or-six-story concrete dorm building. Eight girls of the same class were assigned to share one dorm room. There were four bunk beds in each room. My cousin helped me to set up my mosquito net on my bunk bed, which offered privacy more than keeping the mosquitos out.

Three of the eight girls in my dorm were from Shanghai, one girl and I were from Anhui, one was from Shandong province, one was from Zhejiang province, and one was from Inner Mongolia. We soon became good friends. There were 40 students in our nursing class of 1986, all girls. Most of the girls were very good-looking and attractive. Soon, boys from other classes or even from nearby universities started to have parties with us. After college began, interactions with boys were no longer taboo. Soon a lot of the girls in my class started to have boyfriends.

There were many student clubs in the university. I joined several, one of which was the literature and writing club, and another of which was the psychology club. I was interested in psychology. Apart from regular lessons, there were also a lot of social science lectures given by popular speakers from other universities or institutes. I attended many of those. At that time, China's colleges and universities were open to western democratic ideas. I was interested in those ideas and bought a lot of books by famous western philosophers, such as Friedrich Nietzsche and Bertrand Russell. I also read Sigmund Freud. Those books shaped my developing mind.

Before long, I developed a crush on a young man from Beijing. He was vice president of the student counsel at the university. I met him through my involvement with those clubs. He was tall and very handsome. I fell in love with him the moment I saw him. He was four years my senior. Every time I saw him on campus, my heart would beat fast. I interviewed him and wrote an article for the university's internal newspaper. If I got a glimpse of him one day, I would be happy all day long. But I never dared to tell him that I loved him. I could not handle being rejected. One day, I attended an event held in the university's auditorium. As I sat down in my seat, I saw him sitting next to a beautiful girl wearing a scarf. They seemed to be close. I did not know if she was his girlfriend or not. I was so shocked, it felt as if my heart almost stopped beating. I nearly fainted.

Towards the end of my second year at college, the boy was about to graduate. On most weekend nights, the university's gym would be turned in to a big hall for ballroom dancing, which was popular among Chinese colleges or universities at that time. On the night of one such ball, he invited me to dance for the first time. He told me he was not good at dancing. I was so nervous that I stepped on his feet several times even though I was good at ballroom dancing myself.

One day, he found me in my dorm and exchanged photos with me. He also gave me his address and phone number in Beijing. That summer, my father came back from Yemen, and my step-mother and sister and I all went to Beijing to welcome his return (as his flight landed in Beijing). We had never been to Beijing before. We stayed at the house of one of my cousins. We visited tourist attractions such as the Forbidden City, Temple of Heaven, the Great Wall. I also gave my crush a call and visited his home in Beijing.

Later on, when college started again in the fall, I received a letter from the boy telling me he was going to the U.S. to pursue graduate studies. Studying overseas was a popular goal among Chinese college students at that time. I took a 30-minute bus ride to go to the telecom building located in People's Square to make a long-distance call. (At that time, nobody had cell phones and there were not many places where one could make a long-distance call). I called him and wished him well. I never heard from him again from then on.

Academically, we were studying basic medical courses like other medical school students. The medical model taught was still pretty much a disease model, nothing close to the bio-psy-cho-social medical model the school touted. Some of the courses were difficult. Luckily, I never failed a course. I disliked the nursing courses shortly after I started to take them. The teach-ers placed a lot of emphasis on performing nursing skills and procedures perfectly following a specific order. No creativity was encouraged. I had to learn how to do an IV injection a certain way, strictly following certain steps. We also had to practice making beds; we had to fold the corners of the sheets at a certain angle. Everything had to be perfect. I happened to be a very clumsy person. I was awkward in doing those things, and at the same time, I was not allowed to use much of my brain. I hated it.

However, I was actively involved with other activities on campus. I paid to join an extracurricular English class. The les-sons were given by an old teacher from outside of the University. He was very funny and taught us some interesting things. He picked an English name for me after Shirley Temple, the beloved American child star. Shirley also sounded similar to the Chinese name given by my father. I liked the name and have been using it ever since. I also learned many English songs which were popular on campus then. One of my roommates often played many beautiful English songs. I can still hear the song lyrics "How much is the doggy in the window? The one with the waggly tail..." in my mind to this day.

At one time, some of the girls in my dorm stared to knit sweaters. I also learned to knit. I made myself two nice sweaters. When I went to college in 1986, my father gave me a bank book with 2000 yuan (Chinese currency) deposited in the account. That was a lot of money at that time. I was getting 50 yuan monthly from my father, and that could cover my living expense at the university for a whole month. My father got that money from my aunt in Nanjing; my maternal grandparents had left the money to me through my aunt. That money was for me to spend, so I spent it on buying nice clothes. Since my step-mother seldom bought me clothes as I was growing up, I tried to make up for it then. I frequented Huating Market, a clothing market located on Huating Road near Huaihai Road, the Champs-Elysees of Shanghai. There were a lot of clothing vendors at the Huating Market selling fashionable clothes at reasonable prices, and we could bargain with the vendors to get even better prices. Initially, I did not know much about fashion or how to mix-and-match clothes. I bought fashion magazines such as Elle, which had newly become available. After some trial and error, I found my style. Among the clothes I bought, a plaid light coat was my favorite. I also had a red shirt which I would wear with a white puff sleeve sweater I knitted. With some help from those clothes, I became one of the beautiful girls on campus.

Soon after I started my college life, I learned ballroom dancing, which was very popular at that time. I loved the waltz the most. I loved spinning all over the university gym to the music. I frequented the balls there on weekends. Shortly after my third year of college started, I met a young man at the university ball one night. He invited me to dance. He told me he was a teacher at the nearby Jiao Tong University (one of the top Chinese universities) and that he had graduated from Beijing University, another one of the most prestigious universities in China. We talked and danced until the ball ended, after which he accompanied me to my dorm building and said goodbye.

We started to see more of each other, and he soon became my first boyfriend. He certainly loved me a lot, but I did not really love him as much. Because of the lack of love I received growing up, it felt good to be loved. I rode on the back of his bike, and we went to many parks in Shanghai. He took a lot of nice pictures of me.

Then, at the end of spring in 1989, an anti-corruption and pro-democracy movement erupted in China on college campuses. The students were excited. They posted pro-democracy posters on campus bulletin boards. I became involved as well. I read those posters every day and also joined street demonstrations. We marched on the streets of Shanghai. Lessons were disrupted on campus.

Students in Beijing plus those came from all over China occupied the Tiananmen Square. Finally, Deng Xiaoping ordered the army to clear the students out of Tiananmen Square on June 4th. Tanks drove on the streets of Beijing and on to the Tiananmen Square. Soldiers opened fire on the unarmed students and other civilians there. People died. It was known to the western world as Tiananmen Square Massacre.

As events evolved, I got more and more excited; my mind started to work very fast with all kinds of fleeting thoughts. I lost sleep at night. I recorded messages on my Walkman recorder and asked a friend at the university who had graduated from the same high school to take them to my father. My speech did not make much sense. After my dorm mates all went home, leaving the empty dorm to me, I stared pacing and dancing in my dorm. I wrote broken words such as "Crisis" on the walls of my dorm room with markers. One night, I told my classmates that I could draw a line connecting us to Beijing and that I could speak to the leader of the movement. One of my classmates noticed that things were very wrong with me and reported it to the teachers, who found someone from the psychiatric hospital to see me. This person said I needed to be treated with psychiatric medicine, and that psychological counseling or therapy alone could not help me. The teachers contacted my father.

My father came to Shanghai as soon as he could and took me to my cousin's house. He contacted a military hospital with a psychiatric ward near Wuhu and made arrangements for me to go there. That was the first episode of my mental illness. I was 21 years old. My step-mother's younger brother was the deputy mayor of Wuhu at that time. Through his connections, he sent a car to come to Shanghai that drove me and my father to that hospital outside of Wuhu. I thus began my first mental hospital stay in my life.

CHAPTER 9

I stayed on a secluded mental health ward. There were about 50 patients on the ward. Each room housed about four patients. I was totally confused, disoriented, and out of touch with reality. Doctors tried many psychiatric medicines on me, but none worked. Then they decided to give me electroconvulsive therapy. I remember being taken to a treatment room where the nurse put a padded mouthpiece in my mouth to let me bite down on, feeling the cool touch of a metal electrode to one side of my temple, and then the next thing I knew, I was waking up in the bed in my room. (I don't remember if I had an IV for anesthesia.) I had a total of ten of those treatments. Whether as a result of that treatment or my disease, I lost part of my memory of the hospital stay.

Later on, the doctors finally put me on an atypical anti-psychotic medicine that worked for me. I became more and more coherent. However, the medicine also had some side effects, such as constipation, heart palpitations, and weight gain. After I started to take the medicine, my appetite increased dramatically. I would eat four buns instead of two at lunch and still feel hungry. There was no entertainment or other activities going on in the ward. The nurses just made sure the patients took their medicine. I walked back and forth in the corridor along with other patients. I remember one male nurse touching my nipple inappropriately while taking my temperature under my arm. I reported him to other female nurses. One day, my sister and my boyfriend came to see me. They could not come onto the unit to visit me. I just saw them through the window.

Finally, after over one month staying at the hospital, I was discharged. I went to my home in Wuhu to stay with my father, step-mother, and sister. That summer after I was discharged from the mental hospital, my boyfriend in Shanghai came to visit me in Wuhu. Somehow, I felt he had become a little distant.

My diagnosis at the time was schizophreniform disorder. (Many years later, after I came to the U.S., my psychiatrist changed my diagnosis to bipolar I disorder with psychotic features.) The chaos and excitement of the student movement might have triggered the onset of my illness. However, verbal abuse from my step-mother in my childhood, especially during my teenage years, might also have contributed to it in some way. Later on, I found out from my aunt in Nanjing that my maternal grandmother also had some kind of mental illness, although she never saw a doctor to get a diagnosis and treatment.

There was little awareness of mental illness in China at that time, and great social stigma. It was thought to be a debilitating illness. When I had left home to go to college three years earlier, I was like a bird flying away from the nest. But because of the illness, now my wings were broken. I recall thinking at that time that, if the disease ever relapsed, I would rather die than have to go through it again.

Even my father, as a doctor, did not know whether I would recover from my illness completely and be able to live an independent, normal life. My sister was very kind. She promised my father and me that she would take care of me if I became disabled in the future; that as long as she had food, she would share it with me. I was deeply moved.

I took medical leave from the university and stayed at my father's apartment for one year. I was tired and sleepy most of the day due to the side effects of the medicine I was taking. According to the doctors, I still had to take a maintenance dosage of the medicine for several years. I also tried to study the books my father brought back from my university in Shanghai. I had to study for the four main courses in which I would have to take exams after I returned to university. I had great difficulty studying those books. Probably due to a side effect of the electroconvulsive therapy, I had trouble memorizing anything I read.

Soon it was time to go back to university. I took my exams and narrowly passed them. The classmates I spent nearly three years with had already graduated, while I had one more year remaining at the university before graduation. The last year was a clinical internship, during which we would learn and practice the nursing care of patients in a clinical setting. I had internships at four major hospitals in Shanghai learning medical, surgical, pediatric, and gynecological and maternity nursing in small groups. I did my internship with students of the class 1987. My teammates were very supportive and helped me a lot.

After I went back to university, I went to Jiao Tong University to see my boyfriend one night. He barely spoke to me the whole time I was there. In the end, he walked me to the bus station as if he had never even been in love with me. That was the end of my very first love relationship. He broke up with me out of fear of my mental illness.

I gained about 30 pounds by the time I returned to the university. Some of my previous clothes were too small. I continued to go to the university balls, but I got fewer invitations to dance. Girls who were overweight were considered less attractive in China.

We no longer needed to use ration tickets/coupons to purchase things at the store, but things got a lot more expensive. China went through a period of high inflation during that time. By the time I graduated, my father was sending 100 yuan (doubling the initial 50 yuan) every month to support me. At that time, college students were supported financially by their families, not through working odd jobs, which were not available.

After completion of one year of internship, I graduated from the university with a bachelor's degree in nursing. At that time, jobs for graduates were not openly available on the market. Graduates were assigned to jobs by the government through their colleges and universities. All students from Shanghai got to stay in Shanghai. Good students from other provinces got to stay in Shanghai if they wanted to. Affected by my illness, my scores were not good enough for me to be assigned to a job in Shanghai. I had to go back to Anhui province where I came from. Through my father's connections, I got a job as a nurse at Yijishan Hospital in Wuhu City, where my father worked as the director of the ENT department.

When it was time to leave Shanghai for Wuhu to start my new job, my father came to Shanghai to bring me back. Instead of going by train, we took the passenger ship that operated on the mighty Yangtze River transporting passengers between Shanghai and Chongqing City on the upper stream. (The passage by ship took around 24 hours from Shanghai to Wuhu. China stopped Yangtze River passenger transportation later on.) As the ship departed from the port on Huangpu River (a tributary to the Yangtze River), I looked at the Bund (Waitan in Chinese, the financial center of Shanghai on the western bank of the Huangpu River), filled with its spectacular European colonial style buildings, and bid farewell silently in my heart to Shanghai. I did not know if I would ever be able to come back and work and live in this exciting, dynamic cosmopolitan city again.

CHAPTER 10

I went back to live at my father's apartment. Shortly after, my father was assigned a brand new and bigger apartment, as were given to director-level doctors at the hospital. The hospital provided apartments for the staff at that time. At that point, in China, people did not have to buy homes on the market, the housing market being nonexistent. Housing was instead provided by people's workplaces, although one had to be married to be provided with housing. Unmarried people could only live with their parents or in dormitories. Residents only had to pay a very low monthly fee. We soon moved into a three-bedroom apartment that had a small living room, a bigger kitchen, and a bathroom with a toilet that one could sit on, like those used in America. In the bathroom, we also had a shower for the first time. In the past, we had had to go to the crowded public shower house at the hospital to take our showers once a week in the winters; since while in summer we could take baths at home in big basins, it was too cold in winter to take baths at home since we did not have heating. When the shower was busy, under each shower head, three or four naked women would take showers at the same time. While one put on soap, another would pop in to get a rinse. There was no privacy. I was so happy that we could take private showers at our own home.

I started to work in the oncology ward of the hospital as a nurse. It was my very first job. I was still taking medicine which made me very sleepy in the mornings, making it difficult for me to follow the morning meetings. Other nurses and the head nurse were nice to me. They helped me a lot. There were about 50 cancer inpatients in the ward undergoing chemotherapy. Chemotherapy then was very harsh on the patients with severe side effects, and there were not many effective medicines available to help relieve nausea and other symptoms. Patients had to stay at the hospital to receive chemotherapy. Pain management was also very poor. Patients could only get pain medicine on a strict schedule. Before the scheduled time for the next dose of medication, some patients were in so much pain that they pleaded for pain meds. It was heart wrenching to see those patients suffering from pain, but I was not allowed to give them their medicine ahead of schedule. One of my jobs was to give patients IVs, but most patients' veins were very difficult to access due to repeated chemotherapy. I was a clumsy nurse, not very good at performing those nursing procedures. I also feared that I might gave a patient the wrong medicine by mistake and cause them harm.

I still remember one female patient diagnosed of advanced lung cancer. She was only 26 years old. The first time I saw her, she was very beautiful. But her illness progressed, and after a few cycles of chemotherapy spread over several hospitalizations, she finally died at the hospital, leaving behind a two-year-old daughter. Before she died, she had lost so much weight that she looked like a skeleton. It was very sad.

I worked at the oncology ward for one year. Then, the hospital added a psychological counseling department. I had always liked psychology, so I applied to work there and got accepted. That department consisted of only one doctor and me. My job was to assist the doctor to do psychological assessments of the patients, such as filling out depression scales. It was an easy job and not very busy. I was very happy.

I stayed there for about one year. Then, I heard the news that the head of the hospital had decided to offer a one-year oral English training program to selected hospital staff. The program would be taught by a native English speaker. It was provided free of charge to the students, who would even receive their base salary while on the program. Good heavens! What a great opportunity! As proven later on, learning English would open a whole new world of opportunities for me. I wanted to join. The head of the hospital lived at an apartment one floor above my father's. I knocked at the hospital head's door and told him I wanted to join the English training program. Later on, the hospital decided to select one person from each department. My department, still made up of just two people, also qualified, so I got to join the program.

Soon, the lessons started. My teacher was a 25-year-old handsome young man from Manchester, England. His name was G. He was of the same age as me. On the first lesson, I remember he brought with him an umbrella even though it was not a rainy day, which was a stereotype of English people then. He spoke with a nice British accent. He said he had been working in London and seen an ad from a non-profit organization called Voluntary Service Overseas (VSO) hiring English teachers to work in China. He had responded to the ad and got accepted, and that's how he had become our teacher.

There were about 25 adult students who were doctors or nurses from the hospital in the class, all with various levels of English ability; some barely knew the English alphabet. My English level probably was the best among the students in the class, but none of us, including myself, could speak much other than simple greetings, on the level of "How are you?" I had studied English since the third grade in elementary school all the way up until college. However, we focused on learning grammar and drilled repetitively for taking exams. We never learned how to speak the English language through the Chinese school system.

It was not an easy job to teach such a class. However, G was a great teacher. He taught us three hours every morning on weekdays. We used a book provided by VSO, but G went beyond teaching us by the book. He played games with us and taught us about English culture. I loved his self-deprecating English humor. He taught us about London, telling us about places such as Piccadilly Circus and Trafalgar Square. He taught us about London's cockney accent. He also introduced the English Premier League and the concept of a football pool to us. Every Monday, he let us write down our guesses of which English Premier League team would win. Then, on Friday, he would announce the match results. Whoever in the class made the correct guess would win the jackpot. G would give the winner a prize, such as an English postage stamp or other little souvenirs. He was a fan of Manchester United. Because of him, I became a Man United fan too.

On weekend evenings, he let several of us visit him at his apartment provided by the hospital. He treated us with beer and music. He liked the Beatles and Simon and Garfunkel. His sister came from England to visit him once and brought him some video cassettes of recorded highlights of that season's Premier League matches. We watched them at his apartment. I saw young footballer Ryan Giggs flying all over the football (soccer) field with lightning speed and making goals. It was wonderful.

I studied very hard and fully participated in the class. Before the start of the lessons, I stopped taking the psychiatric medicine that I had taken for the last three years. I regained my energy and was able to focus, and I was back to my old self I was before I was ill with mental illness. I seized every opportunity to practice speaking English in the class and was not afraid of making mistakes. At home, I listened to English radio broadcast channels such as Voice of America every day. I even spoke in

English in my dreams. I also did a lot of reading. I also wrote essays, and G would correct my mistakes.

In addition to attending G's class, I also went to the English Corner at Anhui Normal University (a university training future teachers). People interested in practicing spoken English met at the English Corner once a week in the afternoon. There was a group of American Christian Missionary teachers teaching at the University who would come to the English Corner to speak to those who went there. I became acquainted with them and learned about Christianity.

I am a spiritual person. My beloved grandmother was likely a Buddhist, like most housewives at that time in China. When I was a small child, she told me stories about the Buddha and Guanyin (Bodhisattva Avalokiteshvara), the Goddess of Mercy or Compassion. She also told me about Yanwang (the underworld king) and hell. I just listened, not quite understanding what she said.

When I went to school, they taught me atheism and materialism. The first time I came across the concept of God was through foreign movies.

I loved watching movies since I was little. I don't remember when we were first able to watch foreign movies. I tried to watch every one that was available. We only had several foreign movies to watch in a whole year. Most of those movies were black and white. When I saw churches with sharp steeples and high ceilings and heard holy music played on organs, a feeling of reverence naturally rose in my heart. I saw the cross and the suffering Jesus Christ and Mother Mary, even as such scenes appeared simply as background scenes in these movies. I was deeply moved and felt the strength of God when Jane Eyre said, "Just as if both has passed through the grave, and we stood at God's feet, equal - as we are."

After I got to know those Christian American teachers at the English corner of Anhui Normal University, I started to attend their Bible studies. I started to read the Bible. What bothered me was the idea that salvation could only be achieved through Jesus, that one could not be saved if he or she did not follow Jesus, and that on Judgment Day, people would be faced with the fire of the hell. If God and Jesus were so full of love, why would they condemn so many kind people who do not have the Christian faith to the fire of hell? I hesitated.

That summer, at that same English corner, I met an Iranian-American young man named Kaveh. I was attracted by his speech. Through him, I got to know the world's youngest independent world religion, the Baha'i Faith that originated in Iran in 1860s.

The Baha'i Faith teaches that all religions are from the same God, and Mankind is but one family. It is dedicated to promoting unity in diversity of humankind. It teaches that God loves man and sent a series of prophets and messengers to different people with diverse cultural background at different locations and periods of time. These prophets and messengers used the languages people at the time and place could understand to teach God's teachings. Moses brought laws, Jesus brought love, and Baha'u'llah (the founder of Baha'i Faith) brought unity to Man on the path of globalization, eliminating prejudices and barriers, especially those among religions.

It is easy for followers of religions to become fanatic and develop prejudices towards other religions. Abdu'l'-Baha (son of Baha'u'llah) said in a quote, "Some souls were lovers of the name Abraham, loving the lantern instead of the light, and when they saw this same light shining from another lantern, they were so attached to the former lantern that they did not recognize its later appearance and illumination."

I was deeply drawn to the Baha'i Faith and became a Baha'i. I persist in my independent search of the truth to this day.

After one year of hard work, I was fluent in English. The hospital had a new head who did not renew G's contract, and there was no more English training program. During that year, I also studied a thick study guide for the American nursing board licensure exam NCLEX (National Council Licensure Examination), which was full of difficult English medical terminology. I got the book to prepare for the exam by the Anhui provincial health department to select nurses to work in the Middle East as part of a labor export program. Nurses could earn much higher salaries through being paid in foreign currencies. It was an attractive opportunity for Chinese nurses back then, so I also signed up to take the exam. I put great effort into studying the book and learned English medical terminology that I never learned before.

I was known to be skilled in English at the hospital by the time I finished that one year of study. A fertility doctor at the hospital asked me to be his interpreter to help him communicate with his English-speaking collaborators in Australia. One day, he and another doctor took me to Nanjing to attend a meeting organized by a Dutch pharmaceutical company. That company had a joint venture factory in Nanjing. I interpreted for the doctor while he spoke with foreign senior managers of the company. That was my first time becoming acquainted with international pharmaceutical companies. It dawned on me then that I could also work for these companies. I asked one of the Chinese managers in their Shanghai office who was at the meeting if it would be possible for me to find a job at one of those companies. He said it shouldn't be a problem and gave me his business card. In the early 1990s, China started to attract a lot of foreign investments. Most major pharmaceutical companies set up offices or formed joint ventures in China.

One month later, in February, I went to Shanghai for some personal business. After I arrived in Shanghai, I gave that manager a call, and he invited me to visit his office, where I met a young Dutch manager. The meeting turned out to be a job interview. I was then offered an opportunity to go to their headquarters in Nanjing for further interviews.

I did well in those interviews and was offered a job to work as a sales representative at their Shanghai office, with a salary that was four times what I had been earning at the hospital. I was thrilled. As part of the agreement, I would have to formally quit my job at the hospital. My job at the hospital was a good, stable job which I could work for my entire career without ever worrying about being unemployed. It was a very secure job known as an "iron bowl" job, one that would never break. On the other hand, the new job in Shanghai was not secure at all. I could be fired any time, and there were no guarantees. The open job market had just emerged in China. It was full of unknown risks and uncertainties. But the opportunity of being able to work in Shanghai was too attractive to me. Although Wuhu was a city that was comfortable to live in, it could not compare to Shanghai, the most exciting place in China. I did not want to climb the career ladder at the hospital based on seniority. I wanted the adventure in Shanghai. Knowing me too well, my father fully supported me. He paid the 5000 yuan penalty for leaving the hospital before serving five years after taking the English training program, as had been laid out in the agreement I signed before I started the program. (I was making about 250 yuan a month then.) My father got about 8000 yuan from government compensation for taking the house my grandfather owned in Shanghai. He hid it from my step-mother. After that, I was free to go to Shanghai to start a new job and a new life.

CHAPTER 11

$\mathcal{J}$n April 1994, after quitting my job as a nurse at the hospital, I went to my new company's headquarters in Nanjing for some onboarding processes and training. Then, I checked my luggage and took the train to Shanghai. After I arrived in Shanghai, I picked up my luggage and called a taxi to go to the medical university I graduated from. I paid the driver some extra money to help me to carry my luggage to the fifth floor of the dorm building for graduate students. My good friend Hui, who had been one of my classmates at university, had given me the key to her dorm during my visit in February. I opened the door to her dorm room, which she shared with one other graduate student. Hui was doing her graduate studies at the university. She was not there the day I arrived. I took her vacant bed and sneaked into living in the dorm building. Management of the dorm building was not strict, and they could not tell me apart from any other graduate student, so I got a place to stay for free.

My company's Shanghai office was located in a tall office building by the Bund (the river-front financial center). My job was to visit doctors at various hospitals in Shanghai as a sales representative to promote the company's products. I visited the office once a week. The company paid me to purchase a bicycle for me to get around doing my job. At that time, people rode bicycles on the busy streets of Chinese cities like Shanghai to get around. I was not good at riding a bicycle. I fell several times riding the bicycle after buying it from a bike shop near the dorm where I stayed. It took about 40 minutes to ride from the university to the office. I got a dark tan riding the bicycle to and from my office and the various hospitals in Shanghai.

The doctors were generally nice and not corrupt back then. We did not give gifts of high monetary value to the doctors. My company marketed birth control pills, a women's health osteoporosis medicine, and an androgen replacement medicine in China at that time. I was knowledgeable about those products and could have good conversations with the doctors about them.

I was naturally a good marketer. At that time, China had started to become more progressive, and young women were beginning to have sex before getting married. For the birth control pills, I recommended that the company to market them as providing independence and autonomy for young women. By taking birth control pills, they could take control in their own hands and not have to rely on their partners. I worked with a radio station in Shanghai on a night-time radio program to talk about those topics. In this job, I also got to ride an airplane for the first time. I was a bit scared during the flight, which landed safely. I liked my new job and was doing well.

In the meantime, I lived on campus in my friend Hui's dorm. Another friend named Dong, who was also from Wuhu, was doing graduate studies in pharmacology at the university. One day, he asked me to help him draw blood from volunteers for one of his research projects. One of the volunteers was Dong's high school classmate. Dong had graduated from the rival high school of my high school. This volunteer's name was Shi; he was not very tall, but he was quite good-looking. I drew blood from the veins in his arm many times for the study, and we got to know each other. A few weeks later, Dong invited Shi, some of his other friends, and me to his lab. We killed a few rabbits used in the study and cooked a rabbit-meat meal there.

Shi started to visit me at the dorm room where I lived. He had graduated from another lesser-known medical college in Shanghai and been sent back to Wuhu to work. He had a Shanghainese girlfriend who was his classmate from college. He travelled back and forth between Wuhu and Shanghai to see his girlfriend. He eventually quit his job in Wuhu and came to Shanghai without a job. He had a good friend who was a teacher at my medical university. This friend of his got married and moved out but kept his dorm bed, and he let Shi stay at his old dorm room. Because Shi did not have a job in Shanghai, his girlfriend's family was strongly against their relationship. They broke up eventually, and that girl married someone else, leaving Shi heart-broken.

I was upbeat, and Shi was attracted to me, and he came to visit me more and more often. Shi liked listening to me talk about my work. Later on, I referred Shi to my company, and he joined as a sales rep too. We would ride our bicycles to our new office in South Bund together. (Due to the growth of the sales team, our Shanghai office moved to a new office building.) In summer, Shi taught me how to swim in the university swimming pool. One time, I felt the way Shi looked at me was different when we were at the pool.

Because the university was on summer break, the other student in Hui's dorm did not live in the dorm. I was alone there. One night, Shi came to my dorm and brought a small TV. He liked to watch soccer games. That summer, the soccer World Cup was on. We watched the match together, and he did not leave that night. The next morning, he told me he was serious about me. The problem was, I was not in love with him at all. He was just a friend to me. I was an independent young woman. I did not want to be locked in a serious relationship simply because of having had sex with someone. We were young and both alone in Shanghai. We needed the support from one another. Nevertheless, we got into a relationship that lasted for five years.

Soon it was September, and the new semester started. My friend Hui graduated, and I could no longer stay in her dorm room. I needed to find a new place to stay. I could not stay with my relatives in Shanghai since they did not have the extra space for me. My father also did not want me to ask them for any favors.

I went to a house rental broker market located on Fuxing Zhong Road. It was an informal market run by brokers nicknamed as "yellow bulls" (as middlemen were often referred to in Shanghai). One afternoon, I rode my bicycle there. I saw over ten of those brokers sitting or standing on the side of the street. They had put up cardboard posters listing the information of rooms and apartments for rent. They also had notebooks filled with that information. A male broker approached me. I did not trust him. Then, I saw a female broker. I walked up to her and told her that I wanted to rent a place. She said she had two places that would be a good fit for me, and that she could show them to me right away. I followed her on my bike.

She took me to an apartment complex consisting of several six-story buildings near the intersection of Kaixuan Road and Wuzhong road in west Shanghai. The room for rent was a spare guest room in a three-bedroom apartment occupied and owned by a family of three. They wanted to rent their spare room to make some extra money. The apartment had wooden floors and looked pretty new and clean. The rent was 700 yuan per month, around half of my monthly income at that time. I thought it was decent, and without bothering to look at the other place, I rented the room.

My new boyfriend Shi helped me move my stuff in, and he also moved in himself. Although I did not love him, the two of us needed each other. We were both 26 years old.

After I settled in, I realized it was really awkward to live with the landlord, landlady, and their teenage son. We shared the kitchen and one bathroom. The landlord and his friends often played mahjong in the evenings well into the night, right outside of my room. It was very noisy, and I could hardly sleep. I could not stand it.

We lived there for about six months. Then, one of Shi's friends had a friend who had a vacant dorm room in a dorm building for young teachers at East China Normal University in west Shanghai. Shi and I moved there.

Shortly after we moved into the young teachers' dorm, we got to know the old couple who lived in a room by the entrance to the dorm as the doormen. After learning about our situation, the old lady offered the spare room in her son's apartment near the university. She used to live there with her son, daughter-in-law, and young grandson, but because of her job, she and her husband now lived in the teachers' dorm, leaving her room vacant. She offered to charge us 500 yuan per month to live there. We did not know how long we could live in the young teachers' dorm, so after I saw the room, I decided to move there. It was a very small room, with barely enough space to fit in one queen bed.

In the meantime, one of Shi's friends referred me to join another pharmaceutical company which paid 3000 yuan per month in base salary (three times more than what I was paid at my first company). If I met the sales quota, I would also be paid a bonus. That was very good income. Most doctors only made a few hundred yuan per month at that time. Because of the huge difference in income, some doctors and nurses quit their jobs and joined pharmaceutical companies as sales representatives.

I was one of the first two sales representatives that the company hired. The company was located in a tall office building in the Hongqiao area in west Shanghai. My job was to promote sustained-release morphine for cancer pain relief by visiting doctors at the hospitals in Shanghai. It was similar to what I had been doing at my previous company.

My initial territory was the western half of Shanghai, a huge territory (and was later reduced after more reps joined). I rode my bicycle to visit those hospitals. I remember on one evening, I got lost in an unfamiliar part of Shanghai. (There was no GPS at that time.) On dark streets dimly lit by street lights, I tried to find my way home. I told myself to keep going west, and I eventually got home safely. A few times I fell off my bicycle on busy streets next to big buses. It was quite dangerous.

We had training and meetings in Hangzhou and Beijing. I was familiar with cancer pain relief and acted as an interpreter during training sessions given by English-speaking trainers. There were only a few people in the company who were bilingual and could interpret for those training sessions. We stayed at nice hotels during those meetings and had nice banquets, and I also had my first buffet.

One day, I flew to Beijing to attend our annual meeting. I had exceeded my sales quota and was paid a big bonus. I was excited. For days before I left for Beijing from Shanghai, I did not sleep well. The old lady's (my landlady) son and daughter-in-law with whom I shared the apartment also liked to have friends over to play mahjong at night. The noise kept me up all night. Coupled with the excitement of the meeting, I got into a hypo-manic state.

Right after the meeting finished, I took the train to go to Bangbu, a city in northern Anhui, to visit a key doctor (an opinion leader in the industry). It was a long train ride. I had a lot of thoughts flying through my head. I spoke with strangers who sat next to me on the train. I almost missed my stop. After I got off the train, I took a cab to Nan Shan Hotel, the best hotel in the city at that time. I started to get disoriented. When I arrived at the hotel, I managed to check in, and as soon as I got into my hotel room, I collapsed in bed. I could not go outside of my hotel room to fulfill the purpose of my trip, which was visiting the doctor. I told a hotel employee that I was sick and needed to see a doctor. I waited in my room for a long time and saw a female doctor who worked at the hotel. (At that time in China, some hotels had medical offices for hotel guests needing medical attention.) After listening to my story, the doctor simply advised me to rest and did not give me any medicine. I was so scared. Desperate for help, I tried to dial the phone number to my landlady's son's house, trying to get hold of my boyfriend

Shi. I kept making mistakes and dialing wrong numbers. After trying many times, I finally got hold of my boyfriend.

After realizing I was ill and needed help, Shi bought a train ticket and came to Bangbu. I was very ill with my second episode of bipolar psychosis. When the hotel worker came to my room to fix the TV, I thought they had come to install equipment to spy on me. Shi bought sleeper train tickets to take me back to Shanghai. On the train, I had hallucinations. I heard people on the train talking about me and accusing me. After we got back to Shanghai, I was still very ill. Shi called my father, who told him to bring me home to Wuhu. On the train to Wuhu, I stared at my watch and could not figure out the time. The eight-hour train ride felt like eternity.

CHAPTER 12

*A*fter arriving at my father's home in Wuhu, my father gave me my previous medicine that had worked before. I stayed in bed for a few days and got better on that medicine. I did not have to stay in a mental hospital. After a couple of weeks, I went back to Shanghai with Shi. My manager was nice, and I got to keep my job. However, Shi lost his job at that Dutch pharmaceutical company I used to work for. I took my medicine for a few months and then stopped.

Things kept moving on, and it was soon fall of 1995. One evening, I was at a banquet entertaining doctors and pharmacists from a big hospital within my territory. During a casual chat with my guests, I spoke about my difficulties renting a place to live in Shanghai. Then, the pharmacy director told me he had a colleague whom he could introduce me to. That colleague had a vacant room for rent in downtown Shanghai.

One day, I met with that pharmacy director's friend and his wife at their home on South Shanxi Road near Changle Road, one of the best locations in Shanghai. The room for rent was just across the street on the other side of South Shanxi Road. They took me to see it.

We walked into the lane between rows of two-story townhouses built in the 1930s and entered through a door. We climbed half a flight of wooden stairs in the dark and entered a small room on the back side of the townhouse, in between the first and second floors. The ceiling was low, and the room was small - only around eight square meters, or 90 square feet. It had very old wooden floors. It had one twin bed and a desk. It had better privacy, although I would have to share the bathroom and kitchen downstairs with two other families living there. I liked it very much. The landlord asked for 250 yuan as monthly rent, but the landlady said 250 did not sound good (the number meant "stupid person" in Chinese slang) and told me to pay 200 per month instead. That was very cheap. I could not believe my ears! I felt so lucky.

I moved in without delay. I got to live in one of the prime locations in Shanghai. Just a few minutes on foot south along the tree-lined South Shanxi Road was Huahai Road, the Champs Elysees or 5th Avenue of Shanghai. To the north was the quieter Changle Road. A few minutes' walk along Changele Road to the east was the five-star Jing Jiang Hotel. The Garden Hotel was also nearby.

Although that small room had previously been a storage room or room for the maid, I was very happy to live in it. In the

1930s, some famous writers such as Xiao Hong lived in these sorts of rooms, called "ting zi jian" by the Shanghainese people.

That unit of townhouse was supposed to house one family. However, at that time, it was home to four households. One family lived upstairs with their own bathroom with a bathtub. Shi and I lived in the room in between the first and second floors. On the first floor lived two families - one family of three generations, a grandma, mom, dad, and a grandchild, and another family of a middle-aged couple with a nine-year-old daughter. I became acquainted with the middle-aged couple. They worked as middle managers of a department store. They lived in a 12-square meter (about 130 square feet) room with their daughter. The room neatly fitted a queen bed, a couch, a piano, a wardrobe, and a stereo system. Housing was very tight for people in Shanghai at that time. Shanghainese people are well-known for their skill at making the most out of limited space. The other two families and I shared one small bathroom and a kitchen. Every family had their own gas stove in the kitchen. While I was there cooking, the neighbors sometimes gave me some cooking tips, which improved my cooking skills.

Shortly after I moved there, I saw a job ad in "Xin Min Wan Bao," a popular local newspaper. A foreign market research firm was hiring a market researcher with a medical background. I was interested. It would be a good opportunity to enter a different field. I had been a pharmaceutical sale representative for two years and had learned everything I could learn in that job.

Sales was no longer challenging for me; I was doing the same thing every day. I wanted change. I wanted to work in marketing, and market research would be a good way for me to gain entry into the field of marketing. I applied, got interviewed, and was hired. The 3000 yuan salary offered was less than half of what I made at the pharmaceutical company as a sales rep (base salary plus bonus). I accepted the job without hesitation.

The company was located in an office building above Shanghai's Number 2 Department Store on the corner of Huaihai Road and South Maoming Road. It was only a ten-minute walk from where I lived. I no longer had to ride my bicycle for work. I became a white-collar office worker. On my lunch breaks, I would go window shopping at the department store to check out latest fashions. On South Maoming Road there were many clothing boutiques selling stylish clothing that had been left over from export orders. I would hunt for treasures at those stores after work or on weekends.

I was hired to do market research in the pharmaceutical and medical device markets. My boss was a very nice lady from Northern Ireland. She was based in Hong Kong but traveled to China for projects. We got along very well. I learned to do in-depth interviews after watching just one demonstration. I also learned to moderate focus groups. I learned how to write research proposals, design questionnaires, do analysis, write reports, and make client presentations, all in just one year. I became a good qualitative market researcher, although I did not stay at the firm long enough to learn more about quantitative research.

At first, I did not know how to use a computer or even the copy machine. I often forgot to save my work, and when the computer froze and I had to restart the computer, I would lose all of my unsaved work and have to rewrite everything. (I don't remember if Microsoft Word had an autosave function back then. If it did have one, it was not as advanced as it is now.) I had to work harder. I often worked in the office until 8 or 9 P.M.

I was also preparing to take the test for the MBA program of a joint venture business school (similar to the GMAT test for business school admission in the U.S.). I found their ad in the same newspaper I had found my job in earlier. It was the first business school in Shanghai. Although I did not know much about MBA programs at that time, my instinct told me that it was something I wanted to do. I went to the Foreign Language Book Store located on Fuzhou Road and bought all of the books on GMAT prep I could find. I also attended a GMAT test prep class and received a lot of mock test sets. I studied every day with whatever spare time I could find in my small room.

When I moved into my small room in the heart of Shanghai, my boyfriend Shi also moved in. He did not want to go back to the dorm in the medical university. I did not like that, but I could not turn him away, especially considering that he had saved me in Bangbu when I was struck with mental illness. He asked me to marry him, but I declined. We were from very different background and had different values. I valued honesty, but he tried to teach me to cut corners. He also failed to keep his promises from time to time. While I lived with him, I felt twisted. I never loved him to begin with. My heart grew more and more distant from him.

That small room I lived in was very hot in the summer and did not have an air-conditioning unit. Shi would have a fan on all night. On weekends when I was dedicated to my studies, Shi would lie in bed watching TV all day. We had arguments often. One night, my words upset him, and he left, slamming the door. I wished he would not come back; but he returned the next morning. I told him I was a big, tall tree needing more space and light, and yet he was like vines climbing tightly onto my tree. I did not know how to break free.

During that time, Shi became a sales agent for a Chinese pharmaceutical company based in Wuhan in central China. He took money from my bankbook as his working capital. He got medicines at a steep discount and sold them at higher prices to the pharmacies at hospitals in Shanghai. He would pay the doctors cash for using those medicines on their patients. Such practice was not encouraged by the Chinese government, but it was done by a lot of Chinese pharmaceutical sales agents at that time. Over time, Shi made money and paid me back the money he took from me. Since I had come to Shanghai in 1994, I saved up to 80,000 yuan. That was quite a lot of money at the time, more than my father and step-mother had saved in their entire lives.

In early 1997, I took the business school admission exam. I passed the written test (similar to the GMAT test) and went on to take an in-person interview. I was interviewed by three professors. Later, I received notice that I had been admitted. The MBA (Master of Business Administration) course was an 18-month, full-time course. The tuition was 40,000 yuan, plus a lodging fee of 3600 yuan. I would not have any income over the 18 months of study, and I also had to have enough money to cover my living expenses during this time, as well as to pay for the books. That would use up most of my savings. I couldn't do much with my savings on anything else, but it was enough for my business school education. For me, money was not important; what was important was to learn something useful.

At that time, most people in China had never heard about business school, but I enrolled in the school without hesitation. It turned out to be the best investment I made in my life. Later on, MBA degrees became popular in China, and the business school I went to turned out to be one of the best business schools in the country. The American investment guru Warren Buffett once said, "Investing in yourself is the best thing you can do. Anything that improves your own talents." I could not agree more.

My business school study started in mid-May of 1997. The business school had been established in 1994 as a joint project between the Chinese government and the European Union. As China opened up to the world, there was a lack of talent who understood both local and global markets and the management principles and practices of developed countries. To educate those management professionals was the purpose of the project.

While a new, state-of-the-art campus was under construction in Pudong New District, we studied at the library of Jiao Tong University's Minghang (a suburban district of Shanghai) campus. Our courses were divided into several modules, and each module included four courses. Except for "Chinese Economy" (taught in Chinese by leading Chinese economist Mr. Jinglian Wu), all other courses were taught in English by professors from leading business schools from the U.S. or Europe. Every module lasted for six weeks, and then we would have a one-week break before the next module started. The 18-month MBA program also included a three-month individual internship and a six-week group internship. The study was intense. We studied hard and also played hard. At end of each module, we went disco dancing to release our youthful energy.

There were 120 students in the year of 1997, equally divided into two classes. My classmates came from all over China from different industries. The lessons were taught very differently from those taught in typical Chinese classes, where the teacher did all the talking and students stayed busy taking notes. In classes at the business school (China Europe International Business School, CEIBS), students were encouraged to participate in in-class discussions. We learned through case studies. We also had many group projects. Over two decades post-graduation, I don't remember much of what I was taught then. I only remember that on the very first lesson in "Introduction to Management," I learned that "managers achieve tasks through others." I also learned the importance for companies to reinvent themselves under constant changes in the market driven by technological developments and changes in consumer behavior. I did well in the marketing courses but struggled with courses in finance.

During our studies, we lived in a six-story residential building just outside of Jiao Tong University, rented by the business school on our behalf. We rode our bicycles to get around. Four students of the same gender shared a single two-bedroom apartment. Two students shared one room. I became good friends with my roommate. She got into trouble during the individual internship. She broke the contract she signed with a large international company which was one of the business school's sponsors and took an internship with another big company instead. That original international company filed a complaint against our business school. The school was considering serious disciplinary action against my roommate. We were having business ethics lesson at that time. The professor and the dean were both from Switzerland. I had an idea. I approached the business ethics professor, told him the situation, and proposed a solution - instead of expelling my roommate, we could turn this into a learning opportunity. My roommate would write a case study and make a formal apology to the company. The school management took my suggestion, and the problem was resolved thanks to my creative thinking.

Towards the end of the program, Shi bought me an Alcatel cell phone. It was my first cell phone. We also welcomed a group of exchange students from leading business schools in the U.S. and Europe. (Some of our best students went to top business schools in the U.S. or Europe as exchange students as well.) I became good friends with a young woman from a leading business school in California. Her name was J. She talked very fast and was bubbly. I liked her a lot.

I did my individual internship at a prominent American medical device and supplies company. For the group internship project, I did mine at a top-ten American pharmaceutical company. Before my graduation in November 1998, both companies awarded me job offers. I chose the pharmaceutical company. My salary was over 10,000 yuan per month. It was very high at that time. That was around 40 times my monthly salary before I had left Yijishan Hospital in April 1994.

I also got to move my "hukou" (household registration) back to Shanghai. A Shanghai hukou was very prestigious, as it was official proof of residency in Shanghai. It was tied to the benefits and education system of one of the best cities in China. (Without a Shanghai hukou, children could not go to public schools in Shanghai at that time.) It was very difficult for people outside of Shanghai to get Shanghai hukou. I got it because of my business school education. The Shanghai government had a policy of welcoming talented professionals by offering Shanghai hukou. With my MBA, I was considered one of such talents. When I was born, I had had Shanghai hukou, but it was transferred to Wuhu when I was little. I was happy that I finally got Shanghai hukou again, so that I could enjoy full benefits of living in Shanghai.

The business school I went to (CEIBS) became the best business school in China. The tuition also went up from 40,000 yuan (what I paid in 1997) to 438,000 yuan for the class of 2020. It was no doubt the best investment I ever made in my life.

CHAPTER 13

*T*he pharmaceutical company I joined did a consulting project with one of the leading management consulting companies. As a result of the project, China was identified as an important market with huge growth potential. The company sent a group of foreign executives to lead the Greater China Office based in Shanghai. I became a new product planning manager.

My supervisor was a New Zealander. He was laid back. I got along with him very well. My job was to ensure market preparedness for the company's new products. At the time, the market approval process in China was very lengthy. After a pharmaceutical product was approved in the U.S., it could take three to four years, or even longer, for these products to be approved in China. Clinical trials were required. We held monthly cross-functional meetings with the new product planning, medical, and regulatory departments to give updates on our progress and coordinate efforts to streamline processes to facilitate the timely approval and launch of new products. One of the key new products I was responsible for was a women's health osteoporosis medicine. I met with key opinion leaders (key specialists) in Shanghai and Beijing. The company sponsored these top doctors to attend international medical conferences, and I would accompany them. In doing so, I got to travel internationally. I visited the U.S., Spain, France, Japan, and Singapore on these business trips. The company also provided a lot of training, which I loved.

Later on, my supervisor added market research to my responsibilities. I had two direct reports. I learned to delegate responsibility and trust my team. There was a time when the company rolled out a new performance planning program. Everyone in the company needed to receive training on this. A group of trainers from the company headquarters in the U.S. came to Shanghai to train a select group of local trainers; the local trainers would then conduct training for the rest of the company's employees. I was one of the selected local trainers and was certified to train others. I was doing very well at the company with a promising career.

However, my personal life took a downturn at that time. While I was studying at business school, I was happy to be spending less time with my boyfriend Shi. I broke up with him at one time during my studies, but he chased after me. After graduating from business school, I rented a one-bedroom apartment in the heart of Shanghai on Wulumuqi Zhong Road near the Shanghai Theatric Art Center. Shi did not move in, upon my request. I wanted my own space. He only visited me once in a while. One year later, Shi paid the down payment for a small two-bedroom apartment (purchased under my name, and with me paying the mortgage payments) in a tall apartment building in Xuhui District, a nice area in Shanghai, near a subway station along Line 1. The commercial real-estate market had emerged at that time. I moved in after the space was renovated, as apartments were sold without any interior decoration, and people had to hire separate interior contractors. I finally had my own apartment in Shanghai, but I was not thrilled, since I did not want to marry Shi. I felt trapped. Soon after, I went on a two-week business trip to the U.S.

After returning from that business trip in fall 1999, I found out I was pregnant. On the one hand, I was happy and wanted to have the baby. I was 31 years old, and it was my first pregnancy. I had always wanted to have children. Because my own mother died in giving birth to me, I had always felt a big hole in my heart. I felt that only having children of my own could help me to close that hole. On the other hand, I did not love Shi. I did not feel comfortable marrying him.

I told Shi about my pregnancy and that I wanted to marry him for the baby's sake, but he wanted me to get an abortion. He said he would be too busy with his business to take care of me and the baby. After some heart-wrenching internal struggling, I decided to proceed with the abortion. Being a single mother was just too difficult in China at that time. One of Shi's friends was a gynecologist. This doctor helped me set up the procedure. I had an ultrasound, and the baby's heartbeat was strong. I had anesthesia and did not feel the physical pain of the abortion, except for some cramping afterwards. Psychologically, it was a big blow to me.

While I was still recovering from the abortion, a young woman called claiming to be Shi's girlfriend. She told me to leave Shi alone. I was shocked and did not know how to respond. A few days later, another girl called me saying to let Shi go, or else she would commit suicide. It turned out that Shi was involved in two other relationships. I was fine with breaking up with Shi even after being in the relationship for over five years, but I felt very sad because of the fresh loss of the baby. I was crying day and night and could not sleep. I developed a headache. I thought I might have depression. I went to the Mental Health Center in Shanghai to see a psychiatrist to get some prescription medicine. The doctor did not have my previous health records. He prescribed me some Zoloft (an antidepressant classified as an SSRI). I did not know this was the wrong medicine for me - that due to my bipolar disorder, taking an SSRI antidepressant could cause me to have manic episodes - and took the medicine as prescribed.

I went back to work after taking a week of sick leave. The company was rolling out the performance planning training. As one of the certified trainers, I went on a trip to Suzhou to deliver training to a big group of company employees at a training conference. After I checked in at the hotel, I could not sleep that night. I took several sleeping pills but still could not sleep. The next morning, when it was my turn to give the training, I collapsed. I cried and told the crowd that I had a history of mental illness and was ill. The company developed and marketed mental health medicines and had an employee in the medical department who used to be a psychiatrist. This person asked me a few questions. The company contacted my father and sent me to his home in Wuhu in an ambulance.

My father gave me my old medicine while I stayed at his home. I did not stay in a mental hospital. I got better soon. My company gave me three months leave and told me not to worry about anything. After three months, I went back to work. But things were no longer the same.

The company I worked for developed and marketed one very effective second-generation atypical anti-psychotic medicine, which was same class of medicine as the old generation of atypical antipsychotic medicine I took before, but with fewer side effects. It was very expensive in China. My manager got me some free samples. I took it for about one year. I stopped it due to side effect of weight gain.

For the first few months after I returned to work, I was sleepy during the day and had trouble concentrating. A young man from another product team joined my team, reporting to my boss alongside me. His father was an influential psychiatrist in Shanghai, one of the key opinion leaders the company worked with.

The company changed their management team every three years, so soon my boss was leaving for Hong Kong to assume another position. Before he left, he selected the young man who had newly joined our team to go to the U.S. head-quarters for a six-month training program. If I had not had my last episode of mental illness, I could have had a good chance of been selected instead.

Soon, I regained my energy. We reported to a new marketing director, a Canadian lady. I met with her once a month. I worked on writing marketing plans for products we were assigned.

One day, an HR manager scheduled a meeting with me. She asked me if I would have any problem reporting to a Chinese supervisor. I told her, as long as the manager was mature, it shouldn't be a problem. I did not know why she was asking me such questions.

It did not take long for me to get the answer. My college who had been sent to the U.S. for six months of training returned and was promoted to senior new product planning manager, and I was made to report to him. It was a strange reporting structure. The director position of my department was vacant. I, a new product planning manager, reported to the senior new product planning manager and had a new product planning associate reporting to me. The Canadian marketing director told me that if I had any problems, her door was open, and that I could talk to her any time. I believed her. Later, I also agreed to let my direct report report to my new supervisor instead; however, this was not enough to gain his trust.

My new supervisor had not had direct reports before. Now, he had me, someone with an MBA degree, as his direct report.

He probably was not confident and never trusted me. We were also people with different styles. The company did one training course which classified people into four different colors. He was probably red - someone who liked order and was authoritarian. I was yellow - creative, but did not like to follow orders.

Many of the new products I was responsible for were at least five to six years away from market approval. I did not think we should do too much work on those products, nor that they needed frequent updates. I thought I did not need to visit those specialists too often. Those specialists' time was valuable, and without something substantial to discuss, I did not feel I should go see them. My job was not a sales job. I thought we should focus more on products that were closer to market approval. However, my supervisor had different ideas. He kept pressing me for updates. At one of our meetings, we had a conflict. We disagreed. I lost my composure and left the meeting room. While I passed the marketing director's office, I saw that her door was open, so I knocked and went into her office. I told her I could not work with my supervisor.

The next day, one of the HR managers spoke with me. I realized that HR manager sided with my supervisor. I could not quit because my father was severely ill, and I had to keep my high-paying job to pay for my father's medical expenses. (I will talk more about this in later chapters.) Soon, the company hired my department director, a Chinese manager who seemed to be more mature. Once I reported to him directly, things became a little better.

Shortly after that, the marketing director and HR gave me a position in charge of training in the marketing department and moved my office to a remote corner. There were a lot of training courses offered within the company. Such information could be easily accessible online. However, the marketing director asked me to make a training manual. I made it, and then she asked me to print it out. I printed out about 30 copies using the company's color printer. What a waste.

I became interested in public relations because of my previous work on an erectile disfunction product. I reached out to a public relationship company and was hired as a senior account manager helping the PR firm to grow their healthcare industry business. I worked there for only a few months before being laid off due to the SARS (severe acute respiratory syndrome) outbreak. By August 2003, my promising career in China had come to an end.

CHAPTER 14

While I was working at that American pharmaceutical company, my step-mother passed away due to multiple organ failure in May 2000. She had been ill for several years, and finally she succumbed to her illness. Around the end of September, my father came to Shanghai to see me. One morning, my father told me he had severe abdominal pain. He had a history of gallstones. I called 120 (China's version of 911) and sent my father to Zhongshan Hospital, a leading hospital in Shanghai where I had my internship while pursing my nursing degree.

In the ER, the doctors did some exams and diagnosed my father with acute pancreatitis and a few gallstones in his bile duct. My father was admitted to the hospital. It was a holiday in China on that day. Most doctors were on vacation. A young doctor was in charge, and he recommended ERCP, a minimally invasive procedure to remove the gallstones in my father's bile duct using a scope. My father did not tell the doctors that he had earlier drunk most of a bottle of hard liquor from my refrigerator. I called my sister and told her about my father's hospitalization. My sister and her husband came to Shanghai as soon as they could. The doctor highly recommended the minimally invasive procedure. Wanting to recover sooner, my father agreed to it and had the procedure that night.

The next day after the procedure, my father felt bloated and worsening abdominal pain. The doctor on call was an experienced doctor. He ordered an x-ray and found fluids in my father's abdomen. The doctor ordered emergency surgery. When my father's abdomen was opened, the doctors found he had acute hemorrhagic necrotic pancreatitis, a kind of severe pancreatitis. To make things worse, during the surgery, my father had the severe complication of a duodenal fistula (a hole in the beginning part of the small intestine). My father's condition became critical. He stayed in the ICU for nine days before he was transferred to a surgical ward. The wound on his abdomen was open and never stitched up. He had many tubes in his body. Because of the duodenal fistula, his abdomen was draining a high volume of fluid very day.

My sister (who took leave from her work) and I took turns taking care of my father. We even had to spend the night at the hospital to take care of him. In China at that time, nurses were understaffed, and patients' family members had to take care of all non-medical care. We hired a caregiver at the hospital. Taoma, the lady from the countryside who used to stay at my father's home to take care of my step-mother, also came to Shanghai to take care of my father.

The hospital bill was very high. As a retired doctor, my father was eligible for 95% health coverage by the hospital at which he had worked for his entire career. (The health system was very different in China from that in the U.S. at that time.) However, the head of the hospital changed the rule to discourage retired doctors from working at other clinics or hospitals. They only allowed 70% coverage for those who later worked at outside hospitals or clinics. Since my father worked at another hospital after he retired, only 70% of his medical bill in Shanghai could be reimbursed. I had to pay most of the uncovered expense from my savings. My father and my step-mother's lifetime savings was only around 60,000 yuan and was all used to pay for my father's medical bills. My sister did not have a high-paying job and had no savings. I had to sell one townhouse I bought in suburban Shanghai to pay my father's medical bills. If I could not pay the bill, the hospital would stop giving the live-saving medicine to my father and he could die. I had to travel between Shanghai and Wuhu to ask the hospital where my father had retired from for checks to pay for his medical bills. In the end, we paid over 150,000 yuan out of pocket. That was a lot of money at that time.

After staying at the hospital in Shanghai for four months, my father's condition stabilized. His pancreatitis resolved, but the hospital in Shanghai could not fix his duodenal fistula. My father was very weak. He could not eat anything by mouth and was fed by TPN (total parenteral nutrition). He kept having high fevers due to infections caused by the catheters. When the doctors started him on enteral nutrition (feeding a nutritional solution through a tube inserted into the small intestine), my father had poor tolerance initially and had severe diarrhea. One day, my sister had to change and clean him nine times due to the diarrhea. It was very hard.

I heard a military hospital in Nanjing was good at treating patients with intestinal fistulas. One of my university classmates was working at that hospital as a charge nurse. I took a trip to Nanjing and visited her. She helped me to get a bed for my father. We called an ambulance and transferred my father from Shanghai to that hospital in Nanjing. I sold all the stock I had in the Shanghai stock market at a loss, as the stock market was bearish at that time, and got around 70,000 yuan. I paid all of that money to the military hospital in Nanjing. I also rented an apartment near the hospital, and my sister and Taoma stayed there to take care of my father in the hospital.

The military hospital in Nanjing was indeed very good at treating my father's illness. They used a simple method to block the leakage from my father's duodenal fistula and established him on enteral nutrition. The next step was to get my father stronger through exercise. There were no physical therapists providing rehabilitation therapies to inpatients at Chinese hospitals at that time. A male caregiver from the countryside who was working at the hospital in patient care approached us, asking to take care of my father and help him to perform exercises. We hired him. In the beginning, my father's muscles were all wasted away due to months of being bedridden. He could not sit up in bed without a lot of support. The male caregiver was experienced; he started slow, and little by little, he got my father walking in the hospital hallways. While my father still had a hole in his intestine, the military hospital discharged him. He was to receive enteral nutrition at home and wait for several months for his intestines to heal so that he could have another surgery to finally repair the fistula. By the time he was discharged, my father was climbing 17 flights of stairs at one time.

My father went back to the military hospital in Nanjing to have a final operation to fix his fistula near the end of 2001. Initially, the doctors tried to glue the hole and would not operate on my father. We waited for over a week, and my father grew inpatient. I asked for help from my friend who worked at the hospital as a charge nurse. She told me I should give the head surgeon a red envelope containing around 2000 yuan. (It was not uncommon for doctors to ask patients and their families to pay them a bribe in China at that time.) I felt afraid to bribe the doctor. One afternoon, I found the head surgeon in his office, gave him 300 Euros (equivalent to 2000 Yuan then). Euros had been newly issued around that time, and I had exchanged some money from my French boyfriend. I told the doctor to keep the Euros as a souvenir. I tried to use the novelty to hide my embarrassment of giving a bribe. The doctor did not even look at the money and put it in his drawer quickly, as if nothing had happened.

After I bribed the head surgeon, my father was soon operated on. The surgery was successful. Soon he was allowed to eat by mouth again, after 15 months of NPO (nothing by mouth). My father later told me and my sister one of his weird dreams when he was critically ill. He said he dreamed of Yan Wang (the underworld god). Yan Wang asked him, "Why did you come here?" My father said, "I came to check in." Yan Wang asked Pan Guan (the underworld judge) to check the Book of Life and Death. Pan Guan said, "His name is not on the book of death." Yan Wang told my father, "Go back to where you came from. You still have many years to live." My father then got better each day. It was miraculous.

Later, my father attended my wedding. He also got married again himself. He is in his late 80s now. It is over 20 years after he fell critically ill.

CHAPTER 15

After my abortion, my five-year relationship with my boy-friend Shi ended. I was around 32 years old then. In China, single women around this age were called "female youth of advanced age" (daling nv qingnian). Later on, they were called "left-over women", or "women left on the shelves". It was a derogatory term.

I was beautiful, and I had gotten more mature due to my life experiences. It was the best time in my life. Yet, in China, men preferred younger women who were in their early twen-ties. One of my male classmates at business school once said that women above the age of 30 were "old vegetable leaves." I was so surprised to hear him saying that. I wondered what he himself would be called.

Good men got married early. I did not have much choice. My high-income job worked as a barrier for me to find a partner. Many men in China did not have true self-confidence. They wanted to maintain an advantage economically over their wives. They were supposed to have higher education or social status.

Even though I did not care about those things, it was hard to find someone who would love me.

I wanted a family of my own. I wanted children. I wanted to give my children the love I lacked when I was a child. I could almost hear the ticking of my biological clock. God only gives women a very short window during which they are capable of conceiving. As a flower, my purpose was to bear fruit. However, I had to wait for an insect to pollinate me - a butterfly, a bee, a beetle, some kind of insect - before I withered.

I was a white-collar career woman at that time, but I was willing to give it all up in exchange for a simple life with a husband, children, and a cozy home. To me, my life would be incomplete without having children.

I struggled. I could not enjoy the single life like some of my friends did. I had a few good friends who remained single and lived full and active lives. My father was open-minded and did not pressure me, either. However, I was under my own pressure. I was also worried that my mental illness would keep potential suitors away.

I did not ask for much. All I wanted was an honest man who was confident in himself to love me and have a family with me. But it was so hard to find someone in China for me then.

I asked my friends to help me. I also thought about contacting the popular dating TV show "Dating on Saturday." A friend of mine who taught at the Shanghai Foreign Language University introduced one of her fellow teachers to me. I went on a date with him, but it felt strange. I was not attracted by him. I did not know what he thought about me either. We did not continue dating. I attended some socializing events organized by foreign commercial associations. I dressed myself nicely, but I did not have any romantic encounters.

I had my own desktop computer at that time. I went on Freetel and ICQ (chat platforms of that time) and started to chat with people online. I met with all kinds of people there. Some asked for cybersex directly. But most people I chatted with were okay. I met with a few people offline, but none developed into anything serious. I met one good-looking Texan who spoke fluent Mandarin. As soon as I told him about my mental illness, he changed the topic and cut our date short.

Just when I was almost hopeless, a French gentleman who was a lot older than me started to date me. He was a scholar and quite interesting. He told me he was separated from his wife. He asked for my loyalty, and we stared a remote loving relationship. We wrote emails. He came to Shanghai every two or three months to spend a few weeks together with me. He promised me to get a divorce and marry me. However, he made very slow progress. Maybe the divorce process in France was complicated and he did not want to lose his property and lifetime of savings. After being in the relationship for nearly two years, I decided to leave him. I realized we were at different stages of our lives. I wanted to get married and have children, but this was not a priority in his life. I could not waste my precious time on him.

CHAPTER 16

I was 34 years old and still single. I was wondering whether there was anything wrong with me. Why could I not find a partner to get married and have a family? I started to wonder if God had forgotten about me, or if He was too busy to answer my prayers.

Then, I met up with my good friend J, who was an exchange student at my business school. She lived in the San Francisco Bay Area. She came to visit her father who ran a business in China. When we got together, I told her about my troubles. She told me I could try Match.com.

I registered with Match.com. I managed to pay the monthly fee with one of my credit cards. (I later canceled my subscription after I met my partner.) I wrote a simple profile and filled out a questionnaire. Soon, I received an email. It was from an American man who was traveling to Shanghai on business. He wanted to find someone locally to show him around in Shanghai. I replied. We started to communicate via email. From his emails, I learned that he was working at a medical device company. Since I worked at a pharmaceutical company, we had some common background. He also told me he was a pilot. He could fly single engine airplanes. I wrote to him I was worried about him flying and mentioned French pilot and writer Saint-Exupery, who wrote "The Little Prince" and died in a plane crash. He wrote back telling me flying was actually safer than driving an automobile.

After we had been emailing each other for about ten days, he gave me his phone number and told me I could call him. I dialed his number. He had a nice voice. I told him I was a nurse who was not good at giving shots. He laughed. His name was D, and we talked for about half an hour on the phone. He emailed me to set up a time to meet. We chose to meet on a Sunday in mid-November at 10 A.M. at his office in Hongqiao (a business area in West Shanghai).

It started out as a sunny day, then turned overcast and was a bit cold. I wore a pair of dark purple jeans, a lavender sweater and a light purple jacket. Purple is my favorite color. I wore my glasses and some light makeup and had wavy, shoulder-length hair. I looked good. (I had stopped taking my mental health medicine for about one year, so my weight had also dropped back to normal.) I called a taxi to take me to his office in Hongqiao.

I arrived, found his office, and rang the doorbell. I entered after the door opened and saw him on the phone, when he looked up at me. He wore a short-sleeved shirt. He put down the phone and put on an old leather jacket. Later on, I came to know that it was an aviator's bomber jacket he got as a birthday present from his parents. It was decorated with many metal pins. He was not very tall but was built strongly. He was very good-looking and wore a pair of glasses. We left his office and walked to the first stop of our date - Hongqiao Exhibition Center, to see an art exhibit.

After spending about an hour or so at the art exhibit, I called a taxi and took him to Fuxing Zhong Road and South Xianxi Road, an older part of Shanghai filled with colonial style houses. There were many art galleries in that area. I have always liked to look at artwork. We visited a few galleries and a wedding accessory store that was decorated in an old-fashioned style. At the wedding accessories store, I told him a little bit about Chinese wedding traditions. He listened with interest. He saw I liked a set of sheep family figurines with a mama sheep, papa sheep, and baby sheep. He bought them and put them in his yellow and black backpack that looked like a bumblebee.

We continued to walk north along South Shanxi Road. I walked fast, being used to walking to and from places. He followed. When we had almost reached Huaihai Road, he said he was hungry. We entered a restaurant nearby. We had arrived early; the chef and other restaurant staff were eating their dinners. They welcomed us inside. D ordered pork chops, and I ordered the same. We talked more while we were dinning. I got to know more about him. He was from California and was of German and Italian descent. He worked as a quality assurance manager at a medical device company based in Southern California. The company had factories and offices in China.

Starting three months ago, he had been traveling to Shanghai almost once a month for business.

After our early dinner, we continued to walk. (Later on, D told me he had never walked so much in a day in his life.) We arrived at Shanghai Grand Theater located in the People's Square. He had two tickets and had planned to invite me to a concert. The concert was played by an Australian symphonic orchestra. D liked classical music. During intermission, I told D some things about me. I told him I had a mental illness. He did not seem to be bothered by it. I told him about my troubles with my boss at work (at the American pharmaceutical company where I was working at that time). I said a lot, and he just listened. He also told me more about himself. He was an ex-marine. He had been born in the early 1960s, making him six years older than me. He was divorced.

After the concert, we called a cab. The cab dropped me off at my apartment building in Xuhui district. Saying goodbye at the foot of the tall building, D gave me the sheep family figurines he had bought at the wedding accessory store earlier that day.

Our first date went very well. I did not know if he was interested in me or not; I dared not to think more about it.

The next day at work, I checked my personal email. I had an email from D calling me his dream girl. I could not believe my eyes! I wanted to see him again, as soon as possible. He said he was available that evening. After work, I took a cab from my office in the People's Square to meet him at his office building.

There was a Starbucks on the first floor of his office building. We ordered coffee and found two seats where we could sit down. I looked at his eyes, blue with a tint of green, and saw sincerity and simplicity. I looked into his eyes for a long time, until tears blurred my own eyes. I fell for him. He was the one that I had been waiting for all those years. We held hands and sat there until the Starbucks closed.

We met again the next day (the third day since our first date). He had to go back to the U.S. the following day. I took him to my home, a 77-square meter (around 800 square feet), two-bedroom cozy apartment. I had made the second bedroom a living room. In my living room there was a red sofa bed facing a TV stand. I was nervous and could not find my key, and eventually I had to seek help from a locksmith.

We ordered food delivery from a nearby restaurant and had a candle-lit dinner. I played my favorite music, Celtic Awakening, with the sounds of rain and the running water of mountain streams. D held me as we sat on the sofa enjoying the heat from my space heater. The light from the space heater resembled that of a fireplace. When it was very late, D put down the sofa and it turned into a bed. We held each other to keep warm. Out of respect to me, D did not proceed with more intimate moves. It was a very romantic night. I did not sleep at all. Early the next morning, I called him a cab to take him to the airport. (I had to go to work and could not see him off at the airport myself). Before he entered the cab, D took off his leather bomber jacket and gave it to me. He would be gone for two weeks.

During those two weeks waiting for his return, I slept with his leather jacket, covering my head with it to smell its calming scent. It was a mixture of the scents of leather, tobacco, and aftershave. It was his scent, and it kept me company while he was away. Taiwanese singer Hsin Hsiao-Chi (Winnie Hsin)'s song "Weidao" ("The Scent") kept singing in my head - "I miss your smile, and your jacket; I miss your white socks, and your scent. I miss your kisses, the light scent of tobacco on your fingers; that's the scent of love in my memory."

D was a good writer. He used to keep a journal. While he was away from me in the U.S., I received a copy of his journal entry in my email almost every day. He also wrote me poems. I loved reading those journal entries and poems. In one of his entries, he wrote, "I shall fly an airplane. It will carry the two of us, flying over high mountains, endless deserts, and land in Las Vegas when darkness falls and the lights were turned on." I fell in love with him more because of his writing. (Those were not his exact words; I rewrote them based on my memory, since I lost all of his letters due to problems with Hotmail.)

Those two weeks felt so long. He finally came back. We met up almost every day. One day, he moved from the hotel where he had been staying to my home. We got along very well living together. He liked the food I liked, and vice versa. He liked to eat shrimp. I used to buy live fresh-water shrimp and cook them in the microwave. We would sit at the table peeling those shrimps by candlelight. Sometimes we also ate at local restaurants. There were many good ones nearby. We also went to concerts and even stayed one night at the 5-star hotel Jinmao Tower also known as Grant Hyatt Shanghai (while the price was reduced due to SARS) in Pudong overlooking the Bund. We had a good time.

D was a sweet lover. I loved the sweet little things he did for me. It was a cold winter at that time, and we did not have central heating in Shanghai. Every night, D would lie in my side of the bed first to warm it up for me. I had never been treated with such kind love before. I felt very happy.

One night, after we had been in love for a little less than two months, D gave me a beautiful amethyst ring. He had bought it on one of his trips to the U.S. He told me that the moment he saw me, he wanted to marry me and to spend the rest of his life with me. He asked me to marry him. I was moved to tears.

Later on, we moved to an apartment building behind the Huating Sheraton Hotel. I sold my small apartment. Dean resigned from his job after his company tried to relocate him back to the U.S. He wanted to spend time with me. I encouraged him to start his own business helping American medical device companies to source products in China, but it was not successful. D was an engineer, not so good at selling his business. We then realized that not everyone could be a successful entrepreneur.

During the SARS outbreak, Shanghai's real estate market took a hit. We bought a four-bedroom condo across the street from the Huating Sheraton Hotel. D was not familiar with the process of purchasing a home in China and did not know what he agreed to in signing the documents (all in Chinese). He did not have any money after his divorce. I used the money I got from selling my small apartment and some funds I borrowed from my friends to pay for the down payment and got a mortgage with a monthly payment of around 1000 U.S. dollars.

In the meantime, Dean and I planned our wedding. We went to a professional photo studio to take our wedding photos, according to Chinese wedding tradition. It lasted one whole day. Makeup artists working at the photo studio were busy putting on my makeup and dressing my hair in different styles. I took photos in several different outfits. We went to the Shanghai Bureau of Civil Affairs to get married officially in early September 2003. After filling out some forms, we were issued our red marriage certificate, and the official held a simple ceremony in which we gave our oaths to a dedicated marriage. But that was not all. I wanted a big wedding ceremony.

I made reservation at Xingguo Hotel, a five-star hotel located in the heart of Shanghai, for a date in early October. They offered a western-style wedding, including a buffet in tents set up on their lawn. I sent out invitations to about eighty people. Most of the people we invited were my family and friends. D's family in the U.S. could not attend due to the short notice. We invited some of D's former colleagues at the medical device company he worked for. A couple of days before the wedding date, my father and my sister's family came to Shanghai to attend my wedding.

On my big wedding day, my father, after his recovery from the life-threatening severe pancreatitis and intestinal fistula, gave me away to my husband. My father made a speech thanking all the people who had helped me. D and I took the wedding oath. My brother-in-law acted as our best man. One of my former colleagues at the PR firm acted as my bridesmaid. The two of them presented the rings for D and I to put on.

My sister brought her baby girl to our wedding. After a late-term miscarriage, my sister had finally had another successful pregnancy and delivered a beautiful baby girl.

We also hired a music band to play live music. D and I and our guests danced after the buffet banquet. The guests all brought red envelopes filled with cash, a Chinese tradition to help the newlyweds to cover the wedding expense. It was one of the most memorable days in my life. I was finally married to the man I loved at the age of thirty-five.

After the banquet and dancing was over, D and I got to spend one night at the hotel. We never got to have our honeymoon vacation. Soon after that, D found a job in California. He had to work to pay for the mortgage of our new condo, which he only lived in briefly. Before he left, we started the immigration process to bring me to America.

CHAPTER 17

After a few months, it was time for me to go to the U.S. consulate in Guangzhou for my immigration interview. D came back to China and went with me. During this trip, we also took a short visit to Hong Kong. Without too much trouble, I passed my immigration interview. We went back to Shanghai and bought me a one-way flight to Los Angeles for April 2004.

I met with my parents-in-law at one of D's younger brothers' house. I also visited my childhood pal Jie and her mother Aunt Shen, who had immigrated to the U.S. in the mid-1990s. They lived in one of the satellite cities of Los Angeles. Jie had married a Chinese man who was originally from Vietnam and had two children, a boy and a girl. I was very happy to reunite with Jie and Aunt Shen in the U.S.

My parents-in-law drove me up to their house in Clearlake Oaks, a beautiful retirement community about a two-hours' drive west of San Francisco. Their house was a big two-story house built along a canal leading to Clear Lake, one of the largest natural lakes in California. Their wooden deck sat right on the water. The house had six bedrooms and three bathrooms. My mother-in-law was a second-generation Italian-American and had five kids. She had chosen this big house so that she could have family gatherings.

I planned to stay there for a while to help my parents-in-law take care of their disabled oldest son, Al, while they went on a two-week cruise. Al had had type 1 diabetes since he was a child. He did not take good care of himself and became blind and had other serious complications so he needed dialysis three times a week.

A few days after I arrived and had gotten to know Al, my parents-in-law left. Although Al could not see, he could get around the lower level of the house in his wheelchair. He lived in one of the bedrooms on the first floor. He could get up and go outside of the house to smoke cigarettes or pot. What I needed to do was to check his sugar before meals, give him his insulin shots, and prepare simple meals such as hot dogs and sandwiches for him. Initially, Al was not happy. After a few days, once he realized that I was nice and attentive to his needs, he got along with me better. I spent most of my time reading books from my parents-in-law's collection while Al rested in his bed. Al was the black sheep of the family. He had been in and out of jails for doing drugs or stealing things. D told me Al once stole his birthday present, a brand-new bike, and sold it when they were kids.

After my parents-in-law came back from their trip, D came and brought me down to the one-bedroom apartment he rented near Ontario, Los Angeles. He had been living in the trailer belonging to one of his younger brothers before I came, trying to save money. We had no furniture and slept on a leaky air mattress. When D went to work, I stayed at the apartment alone. D's old car broke down and he bought a new silver Volkswagen New Beetle because that was my favorite car after I saw it at a car show in Shanghai. I had never driven a car in China and could not drive. After D came home, we would cook together. The neighbor's cats sometimes came over. D was a cat person and loved cats. For some reason, those cats liked him. One month later, D came home looking sad. He handed me his last check and told me he had been laid off from his work. He called his mom, who suggested he come up and live with them. We packed up our stuff and drove for almost nine hours to my parents-in-law's house, where we would live for the next three years. We helped to take care of Al while we were there so that my parents-in-law could go on more trips.

The change was huge for me. I had come from cosmopolitan Shanghai to a quiet American retirement community. To adjust to the slow pace of life at my parents-in-law's home, I taught myself to crochet, following a booklet my mother-in-law got me from a thrift store. I had plenty of patience. Stich by stich, I made lots of gifts for my new family members in the U.S. I even made a thread crochet bedspread for my mother-in-law to cover her king-sized bed. She liked it very much.

D and I would frequent local thrift stores, where I search for crochet pattern books and magazines. It was a bargain buying things at the thrift stores. D once bought about ten old 1920s yachting magazines for about ten dollars and sold them on eBay for almost 300 dollars. I also bought a lot of nice crochet patterns and magazines on eBay. We bought a nice Japanese kitchen knife from a thrift store that we have been using to this day. We also bought a Guardian Service aluminum dutch oven which worked wonders for cooking meat.

D and his father both loved fishing. They used to fish on the deck. D caught many big catfish and Asian carp (an invasive species). The Asian carp has too many tiny bones for most Americans to eat. My father-in-law taught me how to fish. I caught several bluegills, but I was not really interested in fishing myself. My parents-in-law had a dog named Milo who was a Jack Russell Terrier. Milo would get very excited every time anybody caught any fish. Sometimes my father-in-law and D put bluegills they caught in a big round bucket filled with water. Milo would go crazy trying to catch the fish. He would run around the bucket and put one of his front legs inside. But the fish were fast in the water and always managed to get away. Milo would bark and bark as he ran around, entertaining everybody that was around. Milo once killed a mallard duck, and we cleaned it and turned it into a delicious meal. There were a lot of snails and crawdads in the canal. D would get into the water and catch those snails and crawdads, and we would add sauces and spices and cook them. They tasted so good.

My parents-in-law also had several fruit trees in their backyard. I got to pick nectarines right off the tree. One plum tree produced so much fruit that I made canned plum jelly. We also went to a place to pick wild blackberries and made pies and other desserts. I learned how to bake from my mother-in-law. We also picked lots of walnuts by the library in Clearlake. I used to sit on the deck and crack the walnuts with nutcrackers.

Once, a neighbor cut down a big tree in his yard. D brought the cut-up tree trunks back and chopped them up into firewood. We burned the free firewood in my parents-in-law's fireplace in the winter, and it felt really warm and nice.

We would drive to the main lake. The lake was very beautiful. In the middle of the lake lay Mount Konocti, a volcanic hill. From the distance at certain angle, Mount Konocti looked like a maiden lying on her back with her knees bent. According to a sad Native American legend, a beautiful young woman fell in love with a young man. After their relationship was broken up by the locals, the young lady drowned herself in the lake. Her tears turned into Clear Lake diamonds (a kind of semi-precious gemstone found in Lake County, California). My parents-in-law had collected some nice Clear Lake diamonds. One part of the lake was called Soda Bay, because the water there was bubbly all year round due to volcanic activity.

Clear Lake was a paradise for birds. Among all the birds, my favorite were the western grebes. Every year during mating season, they would do their elegant mating rituals by dancing on the water. It was simply beautiful. D and I used to go to the lake to watch them.

Soon, I found out I was pregnant. I needed to see a doctor. The U.S. health system was very different from that in China where I could be seen by a doctor the same day. I did not have health insurance. I had to fill out a lot of paperwork to apply for insurance to cover my pregnancy. I had to make an appointment to be seen by a doctor. I got frustrated and said the U.S. healthcare system was so backward. My parents-in-law, who were proud Americans, were shocked to hear me saying that.

I finally got to see a gynecologist. On one of my visits early in my pregnancy, the doctor did a Doppler ultrasound to listen to the baby's heartbeat. She did not hear it and told me it might be too early, since I was about eight weeks into my pregnancy. She said she would try it again on my next visit. On the next visit, she still could not hear the heartbeat. She referred me to do an ultrasound at the radiology department of a local hospital. I went there on the scheduled day, and the radiologist told me he only saw an empty gestational sac. I was shocked hearing that. When I got back, I told D the sad news. D had not been able to take me to do the ultrasound because he was driving for the transportation company that took Al and other patients to and from dialysis. We were both very sad. Soon I started bleeding and had a very painful miscarriage, both physically and emotionally. To console me, my gynecologist told me miscarriages were common and that I could try again to get pregnant in six months. She said that after a miscarriage I would have a higher chance to get pregnant on my next try.

Since Lake County was largely a retirement and tourist county, there were not any local jobs in D's area of expertise. It took him nine months to get a contract job in Sacramento. The commute was two hours each way. Later on, he had another contract job in Santa Rosa. He had to drive the winding mountain roads for over an hour to get to work. He would leave early in the morning when it was still dark and come back late in the evening. Before and in-between those contract jobs, he did odd jobs such as driving for the local medical transportation company or working for one of his cousins who had a tree service company.

We had to make mortgage payments for our condo in Shanghai. We had not rented it out before we left. I had to work to help make those payments and to support us. My first job in the U.S. was to work at the fast-food chain Jack in the Box. I learned how to make French fries and fill orders and work as a cashier to take orders. It was a busy job that I had never had before. I worked there as a part-time employee for about 3 months.

In the meantime, my mother-in-law's younger sister aunt C, who was a caregiver for disabled people living in group homes, brought me information about a CNA (certified nursing assistant) training program at a local nursing home. The nursing home was recruiting a group of students to be trained to become CNAs while working at the nursing home. Students were paid minimum wage while working and receiving training on the program. Although I had a four-year nursing degree in China,

I did not have an RN license and could not work as a nurse in the U.S. I enrolled in the training program. I received training in CPR (cardiopulmonary resuscitation), taking vital signs, transporting patients safely, and so on. At the end of the three-month course, we had to take a CNA exam, which included a written test and a skills test, on skills such as taking vital signs. I passed the exam and got my CNA certificate.

Working at the nursing home was very hard work. One CNA would take care of five to six residents. Half of the residents in the nursing home were coherent and more independent. They got to participate in activities such as playing bingo or other games. The other half were not. Most of them had dementia or other severe illnesses. They needed a lot of nursing care and assistance. Caring for them was difficult. I remember caring for one resident who could not speak due to a stroke. She wanted things done in certain ways, but she could not speak. She got very frustrated when I could not do things the way she wanted. I kept trying and finally figured out what she wanted, and then she was happy. There was one elderly African-American woman with advanced dementia who did not know what was going on around of her anymore and could only make noises that were unintelligible. I assisted her to take showers, and it was very difficult to clean the stools stuck on her bottom. It was really hard work - the hardest job I've ever had in my life.

Soon, I found a job ad in local pennysaver: Lake County Record Bee's Penny Slaver. Lake County Tribal Health was hiring a diabetes education assistant. I applied and went through several rounds of interviews and got hired. It paid a little higher, and the work environment was a lot better. It was also a much easier job. My job was to assist the registered dietician and public health nurse to provide diabetes education services to the local tribal population. We went on outreach programs to visit tribal people in their communities and did free glucose screenings. I also helped organize the annual tribal sports event. I loved my new job. I worked there for three months but resigned in anticipation of a relocation to Sacramento due to D's new job. However, D's contract was terminated unexpectedly, which ended our plans for relocation. I also found out I was pregnant again.

CHAPTER 18

*M*y new pregnancy seemed to be progressing fine, and as it was my second one in the U.S., I was more familiar with navigating the healthcare system. Now, I would like to talk more about my in-laws.

My father-in-law was in his mid-70s. He was a U.S. Air Force veteran who fought in the Korean war. He had made a career as an engineer working for NASA. He was involved in the Apollo projects. My husband was very proud about his father's work. My father-in-law was a very down-to-earth person. He was born and raised on a farm in Arkansas. He did not talk much about his previous work. He liked to talk about the weather and fishing and would joke about things that happened on the farm in Arkansas. He had a southern accent that I had trouble understanding. He was a Republican and NRA member. He was frugal. D and I living at his house probably caused a lot of stress on my father-in-law.

I consider myself a moderate-leaning Democrat politically. I was attracted to democratic ideas. I did not like President George W. Bush, who got the U.S. into the Iraq war based on so-called "weapons of mass destruction." I liked to watch CNN and MSNBC. My parents-in-law usually watched Fox News. I liked to watch political commentator Keith Olbermann's Countdown show on MSNBC, which sharply criticized the Bush administration. My parents-in-law probably did not like it, but they were too kind to tell me.

My mother-in-law was in her late 60s. She was a second-generation Italian-American. Her father came to the U.S. as a teenager to avoid World War I. He went into the restaurant business and owned restaurants in San Francisco Bay Area and finally settled in Lake County where my mother-in-law grew up.

I got along very well with my mother-in-law. She was the best mother-in-law I could have asked for. She never intervened in my life with my husband. If we needed support, she was always there for us. She liked to listen to me telling her about things in China. She asked me many questions. Sometimes she would mix up Shanghai with Singapore. She was an open-minded American lady.

Seeing me so sad after my miscarriage, my mother-in-law gave me a beautiful bracelet made of tiny frogs that she had bought on one of her trips, as a token to wish me the good luck of frogs that produced many babies. It probably worked, since I became pregnant shortly thereafter.

My mother-in-law was generous and did not care much about money. She liked to play slot machines at the casinos. There were three casinos locally which she frequented with my father-in-law or her younger sister, Aunt C. She also liked to go to Reno to play at the casinos there. Shortly after I arrived, she took me to a local casino. I had never been to a casino before. She gave me a 20-dollar bill to play with on the penny machine. I played very carefully, trying not to lose that money. I was taught not to gamble by my grandmother. That was the only time I ever played at a casino.

In the summer, D's sister and brothers would bring their families to visit my parents-in-law. D's sister and her family lived in Oklahoma. She dedicated her life teaching kids about nature and received many awards, including an award issued by President Obama. She had two beautiful daughters. While I was six months pregnant, D and I took a flight and visited them in Oklahoma. While we were there at their house, my sister-in-law invited several of their neighbors to welcome me. They asked me to tell them some traditions related to childbirth in China. I told them that when babies were born, parents would give friends and family eggs dyed red, and that giving an even or odd number of eggs would tell the gender of the baby. That's a tradition from the part of China where I was from.

D's teenage son from his previous marriage also came to visit D and his grandparents a few times while we were there. He was a very nice young man. When he was here, I tried to let D spend as much time with his son as he could and tried not to get in their way.

After we came back from Oklahoma, my mother-in-law's doctor found that her lung cancer had returned. She had had lung cancer about six years prior and had surgery that removed part of her lungs. She had tried to quit smoking but failed. Her cancer was small-cell lung cancer. It was not operable but sensitive to chemotherapy. Her doctor recommended both chemotherapy and radiotherapy. Fearing the side effects of radiotherapy, my stubborn mother-in-law refused it. She only accepted chemotherapy after she was persuaded by her children.

After chemotherapy, my mother-in-law was very sick. She rested in her bedroom, but she never asked me for help. When she felt better, she cooked her own meals. She still went to the casinos whenever she felt better. She lost her hair and bought some wigs. I crocheted her some hats, and she liked them.

While my mother-in-law was doing chemotherapy, my pregnancy progressed, and I became close to labor. D and I took Lamaze birth classes to learn breathing techniques for labor and delivery. I also used D's grandmother's sewing machine, kept by my father-in-law, to make my baby a small baby blanket using soft flannel fabric I found at the thrift store.

As I got closer to my due date, I started to have more frequent contractions. My husband drove me to the hospital in Lakeport. The nurses checked my cervix, and it was 2 centimeters dilated. I stayed at the labor center overnight for observation. The next morning, the nurses found that I had not made any progress. They spoke with the doctor, who decided to send me home.

After I arrived home, I was very worried. I called my childhood pal Jie in Southern California. She told me to call the doctor and ask him to take some actions to speed up my delivery. I asked the doctor to do a C-section before, but he declined, insisting that I could have a vaginal delivery. I called the doctor's office telling them my concerns. The doctor finally agreed to have me come in the next day for an induction.

My nurse was from Eastern Europe. She gave me an IV of Pitocin and later medicine to soften my cervix. She encouraged me to walk around the room. I also sat on a big ball while holding on to the side of my bed as directed by the nurse, to help facilitate the labor process. At around 8 P.M., my cervix was dilated to 4 centimeters, and I started to have very strong labor pains. With every contraction, the pain was so intense that I squeezed D's hands. The nurse asked me if I wanted to have an epidural. I agreed. The nurse called the anesthesiologist, who came shortly and successfully placed the epidural. My water also broke at the time of the epidural. It turned out to be a good decision. The pain was largely reduced, but I still could feel the urge to push and the pressure of baby's head descending.

Close to midnight, the nurse found my cervix was fully dilated. She called my doctor. The doctor came and checked me. He asked me to push. I used the breathing techniques I learned from the Lamaze class while I pushed. D was so nervous that he forgot to count for me. I reminded him to count. After a few pushes, the baby's head was showing. The nurse let me touch my baby's head and brought me a mirror for me to see. The doctor asked me to continue to push. After a few more pushes, the baby's head and body came out, and I heard loud cry. I was overjoyed. I also felt relieved and said so aloud. D cut the baby's cord, and at the age of 38, I became a mother the first time.

The nurse showed me the baby. I exclaimed, "He looks like me!" The baby had lots of black hair. It seemed that my Asian genes were dominant. After the nurse cleaned the baby and did some initial exams, she handed me the baby for skin-to-skin time. The baby successfully latched on. The next day, a La Leche League certified lactation nurse came to see me and taught me more about breastfeeding. I fed the baby on demand. I successfully breastfed my baby until he was one year old.

We named our baby R after our favorite Manchester United soccer player. We were discharged two days later on a sunny day.

R was a healthy baby and grew fast. We had some more good times at our parents-in-law's Clearlake Oaks house. After chemotherapy, my mother-in-law's lung cancer went into remission, and she and my father-in-law went on more trips while D and I took care of Al.

D tried to teach me how to drive. I was clumsy and kept driving into bushes. The first time I took a driving test, I failed the test by backing up onto the curb. Later on, my mother-in-law recommended that I take driving lessons from a professional driving school. I took the lessons but still did not feel confident. On my second driving test, I passed, to my surprise. But I never felt comfortable driving. This was one of my biggest deficits living in the U.S. Without being able to drive, I was like a handicapped person who could not get around freely and independently. The U.S. did not have a good public transportation system like China.

When R was 8 months old, D and I took him to China. We lived in our condo in Shanghai for a short time while trying to rent it out. We found a tenant. The rent would cover our mortgage payment. We also took R to Wuhu to see my father and my sister. Everyone loved R. I also met with my friends. One of my friends who worked at an American pharmaceutical and medical device company said she would help me to find a job at her company. I agreed.

I went back to the U.S. in January 2007. Both D and I saw R took his first step. It was wonderful. My friend made arrangements. I had phone interviews and also an in-person interview with a department head who was on a business trip in San Francisco. D took me to San Francisco for the interview. I was offered the job. In the meantime, I found out I was pregnant again. Thinking that it would be too much burden to my parents-in-law if we continued to live in their house with two babies, I accepted the job offer. D, R, and I moved back to Shanghai in March 2007.

CHAPTER 19

*W*e flew to Shanghai and moved into a three-bedroom apartment in Pudong District that my friend Yan rented for us in advance. My sister also brought Taoma, her daughter's nanny and the former caregiver to my step-mother, to help us take care of R while I worked.

Taoma was a good nanny to R. She looked after him while I went to work and did cleaning and cooking. We paid her a decent salary, several times more than she was paid by my sister in Wuhu. She was from the countryside outside of Wuhu city. As a farmer in China, she only had a small piece of land that could not produce enough income to support her and her family. Her husband died in a motor accident. She raised her four children on her own. Later on, she came to Wuhu to work as a caregiver. She worked for my step uncle and aunt. After my step-mother got very ill, my step-uncle and aunt sent Taoma to take care of my step-mother and she stayed with my family, taking care of my father, my sister and her daughter.

I worked at the American pharmaceutical and medical device company my friend referred me to. I was a senior product manager for the company's glucose monitoring system (glucometers and test strips). I was responsible for updating marketing messages and materials and answering product-related questions from the sales team. I worked there for about seven months before I gave birth to my second son, S.

About three weeks before my due date, at one of my prenatal visits, the doctor asked me to check into the hospital. I chose one of the top maternity hospitals in Shanghai. It was affiliated with my university, and I had had my internship there while I was studying for my nursing degree. My good friend Yan worked at the hospital. The second day after I checked in to the hospital, the doctor found the baby's heart rate was a little abnormal and sent me to labor and delivery unit to get ready for an induction. I stayed there for about four days before the doctor did a C-section. They did not do epidurals at the hospital at that time. Fearing the labor pains, I asked Yan to ask the doctor to perform a C-section.

On the day of the surgery, my husband was asked to sign consent forms (written in Chinese) which he could not read. My sister came to Shanghai to help us. After meeting with D briefly for the consent form, I was brought into the labor and delivery unit and soon taken to the operating room. I was very scared. I feared that I would not be able to come out alive. D was not allowed to come into the OR. Luckily, the surgery went smoothly, and the baby was taken out of my womb. I heard his cry, not as loud as R's when he was born. The nurse showed me the baby briefly above my head. All I could see was the baby's tiny feet.

After the surgery, I was brought to my room. I paid extra to stay in a single-patient room. After the anesthesia wore off, I felt severe pain. The doctor did not give me any pain medicine. The severe pain lasted several days. We named the baby S, an Irish name. S stayed in the nursery for a couple of days and then was brought into my room. I started breastfeeding, and again it was successful.

Before I gave birth to S, we also found a buyer for our condo through a real estate agency. We sold it for almost twice our purchase price. It had almost doubled in less than four years. I wanted to sell it because I was worried about the risk of me dying from childbirth. The chance was very low, but if it happened, it would have been very difficult for D to sell the house and get the money out of China. If we had not sold that condo, its market price would now be a couple million U.S. dollars (more than triple or quadruple) due to the absurd growth of China's real estate market.

After we sold the condo, I put the money into the Chinese stock market, which was doing very well. A good friend of mine worked at a security trading company, and she introduced me to a broker who agreed to help me manage my investment portfolio on my behalf. I did not know much about stock investment even with my business school education. My stocks did well initially, but after the financial crisis in 2008, we lost a lot of money, nearly all of the appreciation of the condo. I was too naïve and should not have trusted someone else with our money. It was a big mistake, and I learned a lesson with a hefty price. D did not blame me for this.

After I finished my maternity leave, I decided not to return to work. I wanted to spend more time with my babies. I resigned. Things were much more expensive due to inflation. However, D landed a good-paying contract job in Suzhou (a historic and also industrial city near Shanghai) with a UK company.

When S was around four months old, my mother-in-law flew over from San Francisco to see her new grandbaby. She was in-between chemo cycles. She was experiencing side effects and felt tired, but she made the effort to come to see us. She was very happy to see her grandsons. I took her to the Yu Garden (Yuyuan) in the heart of Shanghai. I also took her to the Oriental Pearl TV tower to get a panoramic view of Shanghai from up high. When she saw the view of endless skyscrapers, she told me it was "intimidating." Old houses in Shanghai had been knocked down to build tall buildings, office buildings to rent to businesses and expensive condos for people to purchase as homes or investment properties. At one point, it was said that three-fourths of the world's specialized cranes to build high-rise buildings were at construction sites in Shanghai. Similarly, such construction also happened in almost all of the cities in China, including Wuhu. Old houses were taken down, farm land was sold to real estate developers, new apartment or commercial buildings were built everywhere, and housing price kept rising.

We took my mother-in-law to a seafood restaurant near where we lived. We also booked a hotel room in the Jinmao Tower for her to enjoy the view of the Bund at night, lit by beautiful lights. She went back to the U.S. after about two weeks. Before she went back, I also took her to the market at the Pudong subway station, where she had fun bargaining with the vendors to buy gifts to take home.

D started to commute to his job in Suzhou via subway and train. I rented a three-bedroom apartment in Kunshan, a smaller city next to Suzhou. We moved there when S was around 8 months old. We bought a minivan for D to drive to and from work. The air quality was very poor due to heavy pollution; the sky often appeared orange due to smog. The boys were sick often. The apartment was on the first floor of a six-story building. It had a small backyard, and Taoma planted vegetables such as bok choy there. She used a bucket to save the boys' urine and diluted it with water to fertilize the vegetables, something Chinese farmers had been doing for thousands of years. When D found out about it, he was utterly surprised.

R was two and a half years old, but he could only speak a few words. I became worried. I took him to see specialists in Nanjing and Shanghai. They did not give us any diagnoses. I sent R to a local preschool. R liked to sneak out of the apartment. One such day he sneaked out, Taoma and I were busy watching S and did not notice. Luckily, D came back from work and found R outside and took him home. We could have lost him forever if he had been picked up by others. In China, it was not uncommon for children to be stolen and sold to people who wanted children. That was the best luck I had in my life.

I had stopped taking my mental health medicine for nearly seven years. The stress of worrying about R's development took a toll on me. I could not sleep for days and had psychosis again. I was disoriented. Kids' TV shows sounded strange and scary to me. In my hallucinations, I thought I saw the back of God, who told me to follow Him. I became totally incoherent. My sister came and brought me to her apartment in Wuhu. They were not able to take care of me safely, so they had to send me to a mental hospital on the outskirts of Wuhu. That was my second hospitalization due to my mental illness.

The hospital ward was locked by iron gates. I remember being tied to the bed. I asked the nurse to untie me so that I could go to the bathroom. I got no answer and peed on myself. It was a cold November day. I also missed S's first birthday. S had to wean off from breastfeeding abruptly. Luckily, we had Taoma and my sister's help. D traveled back and forth from Kunshan to Wuhu and lost his contract job. It was very difficult, especially for D. He did not speak the Chinese language and had no one to really talk to. I had told him about my mental illness before, but he never knew how bad it could actually be until then. He did not know whether I would be able to recover ever again.

After taking my old medicine, I got better and was discharged from the hospital after about 20 days. Following my discharge from the hospital, I went back to Kunshan with Taoma and the boys. I travelled to Shanghai once every month to see a psychiatrist. I switched to a newer medicine with fewer side effects (the one I took before when I worked at my first American pharmaceutical company). However, it still caused significant weight gain. One year later, I felt very thirsty and was diagnosed as having type 2 diabetes. I was prescribed diabetes medicine.

D started to look for jobs. After a few months, he got an interview. He flew to the U.S. for the interview and was later offered a job in northern New Jersey. Using the money we got from the sale of our condo, which was still left after the loss in the Chinese stock market, we booked one-way flight to go back to the U.S. We said goodbye to Taoma and my sister and my dad. Initially, we planned a stop at San Francisco to see my parents-in-law. However, at the airport, we found out that we needed to go through a process to verify S's nationality. I had overlooked this requirement by Chinese government. We had to stay at a hotel in Shanghai for a week to get clearance. We canceled our flight and booked another to arrive via New York's JFK airport instead. D had a set start date, so we could not stop over in California after losing one week's time. In March 2010, we bid farewell to Shanghai and returned to the U.S.

By the time we left, China had had tremendous development due to the Open Door policy and the hard work of the Chinese people. It had become one of the world's more developed countries, even though people in some parts of China still remained poor.

CHAPTER 20

*O*ur trip from Shanghai to New York was a difficult one. When we boarded the plane, R started to cry very hard. It took quite some time for him to stop and calm down. Later on, R crawled all over the airplane under people's seats. I had to chase him down. It was a long flight. S threw up on me upon landing. Finally, we arrived at JFK airport in New York City safely. My friend L's husband picked us up and drove us to their home in Scarsdale, NY. We stayed there for about a month, during which D went on a business trip to Sweden. After D came back, he rented a three-bedroom apartment in Mahwah, New Jersey (northern New Jersey), and we moved there.

R still did not speak many words at the age of four. My friend L recommend that I contact our local school district for an evaluation. Her son had been diagnosed with autism and was receiving services. I wasted no time in reaching out to our school district. R was evaluated. A specialist doctor diagnosed R on the autism spectrum. The school district determined R was eligible for special education services. While R was being evaluated, the teachers noticed that two-year-old S was not speaking much either. They recommended that we contact early intervention. Soon R started going to special education classes, and we started to have a teacher come to our home to do early intervention sessions for S. I also found a BCBA (ABA therapist) who developed a home therapy program delivered by an ABA therapist's aide for R, in addition to school services that we paid for out of pocket. After S turned three years old, he started half-day preschool at our school district.

We were lucky again. New Jersey happened to be a state offering some of the best special education services for children on the autism spectrum. With proper intervention, both R and S made significant progress. They both became verbal. After S graduated from preschool, he was declassified, meaning he could attend general education classes. R did not need to go to autism classes anymore. He would attend self-contained special education classes for kids with various disabilities.

I saw a primary care physician who prescribed me mental health medicine (the same one I took in China) and diabetes medicine. That mental health medicine made me sleepy. When the boys went to school, I slept in. I did not work. Raising two young children kept me busy.

After working at his company for nearly three years, D got a new boss whom he could not stand and resigned. It took him almost eight months to find another job in central New Jersey. At first, D worked weekdays at his new company and stayed at nearby hotels. He came back on weekends. After summer started, we were planning to move to somewhere within commuting distance to D's new job. Through our private BCBA, I found a consultant who was familiar with the special education services of central New Jersey school districts. We paid the consultant for her opinion. She recommended a few school districts. I searched homes for rent on Zillow in those towns. When D went to see the homes, he liked the first one he saw and signed a lease agreement. Soon, we all moved to the three-bedroom house in South Brunswick township in central New Jersey, a 15-minute drive north from Princeton.

We all liked the new house. It was a one-story ranch-style house with a big front yard and a fenced-in backyard. There was a shed where D spent most of his time reading the newspaper and listening to the radio.

D and I got along very well. My English was good, and we did not have many communication barriers. One time, we did have a miscommunication that was actually funny. We drove by a building with a sign for a "Wet T-shirt Contest." Thinking how D often wore wet t-shirts to stay cool in the summer, I told D he would win the contest if he participated. D laughed. He then told me that wet t-shirt contests were for women to show off their curves. I was totally clueless.

Like most women, I was a multitasker. However, D could only handle one thing at a time. He felt overwhelmed when I told him about several things in one conversation. He would become upset. I did not know why until I read the book "Why

Men Don't Listen and Women Can't Read Maps: How We Are Different and What to Do About It" written by Allan and Barbara Pease. I started to tell him one thing at a time, and it seemed to work.

D did not like to travel, so we spent most of our time at home. We only took the boys to nearby places. D taught the boys fishing at local ponds and canals. We never got the chance to go back to northern California to visit my in-laws again. My mother-in-law's cancer returned. She could no longer take care of Al. Al was sent to a local nursing home where he died. My mother-in-law was heartbroken. Like in the Chinese saying "persons in silver hair burying the ones in black hair" (referring to parents burying their children), it was one of the saddest things in life. Shortly after, my mother-in-law passed away due to advanced lung cancer.

As recommended by my new primary care physician, I started to see a psychiatrist who diagnosed me as having bipolar I disorder with psychotic features. He managed my condition by prescribing psychiatric medication. I asked about newer medicine with less side effect of weight gain. He switched me to one of those newer medicines.

After we moved to our new home, R and S went to local schools. They were very good schools with excellent special education programs. After kindergarten, S was found to have an attention deficit disorder. His teacher used special ways to keep him focused. When he was in fourth grade, I took him to see my psychiatrist, who put him on ADHD medicine. When S was in fifth grade, the school child study team determined that S had Asperger's syndrome, a kind of high-functioning autism, with challenges in social interactions. Nevertheless, with the help from dedicated education professionals, they are to this day learning new skills and making progress. They are wonderful kids.

My boys continue to grow. They turned out to be loving boys with good senses of humor. R loved nature. He liked to draw. He had the positive attitude of "if you get lemons, turn them into lemonade." One day, D caught a beetle to show the boys and then released it into the backyard. S was worried about the beetle. I heard R telling S, "Don't worry - he will find his true love."

S was quick in learning new ideas. He liked science and video games. He had the idea of establishing a "save the animals team," but he did not know how to do it. He asked me one day, "Will I become famous?". I told him there were pros and cons of being famous. I did not know if he fully understood me. One day when I felt sick, S brought me a pillow and asked me if I wanted some warm water with honey (something he always had when he was sick). He told me, "Mom, I will stay by your side in case you need anything." It felt so sweet.

The boys got along very well. They played together and kept each other company. I hope they will continue to look after one another after they become adults. R was good at art, and

S started to learn the violin. Now they are 13 and 14 and have grown much taller than D and I.

After living in the house for a couple of years, we decided to purchase a home. We knew the owner of the house we were living in wanted to sell it. We spoke with a local real estate agent who showed us a few homes. After some comparisons, we still liked the house we were renting best. We decided to reach out to our landlord to purchase the home we were living in to avoid the trouble of moving. The house was built in the late 1950s and had been updated by our landlord. The price was affordable to us. The landlord gave us a few thousand dollars' discount, which covered the cost of replacing the roof, which was too old and starting to leak on raining days.

We became homeowners in the U.S. We planted a peach tree, a cherry tree, and some berry plants in our yards. They produced fruits and berries for us to enjoy a few years later. I bought wintersweet trees online and planted them. Those were common flowering trees ("la mei hua") in the area of China where I grew up. They produce tiny yellow fragrant flowers in January, in the middle of the winter. I loved the scent of those flowers and would cut some branches with those fragrant flowers and put them in a vase in my office to enjoy their beautiful scent.

We adopted a female kitten from local animal shelter. D loved cats, and my grandma had loved cats. It soon grew into a big fluffy cat weighing about 13 pounds. She was a Maine Coon mix. D raised her as an indoor cat. She brought a lot of fun to us. We all loved her dearly.

I got a smartphone. On a friend's suggestion, I downloaded the popular Chinese social media App WeChat. It made communicating with my friends and family in China easy. I had weekly video chats with my sister and father in China. I joined a few groups, such as groups of my high school, college, and business school classmates. I chatted with my friends both in these groups and individually. One of my high school classmates who was great at writing encouraged me to write. I said that I could not write. He told me, "If you can speak, you should be able to write." Feeling encouraged, I started to write blog articles. One of my friends at college introduced me to Wenxuecity.com, the biggest overseas Chinese website. I created a blog there. I wrote blog articles based on my life stories. It turned out I was quite a good writer in Chinese and got many reads. Some of my readers contacted me, and we became friends. My blog articles also formed the basis for this memoir.

After Xi Jinping came into power, China's ruling party, the Chinese Communist Party, tightened control of people's communications. They put a lot of effort into censoring people's posts or chats on the internet, including on the WeChat app. Some of the groups I joined were closed down because the chats contained sensitive words. In order to escape from the censorship, Chinese people became creative with the Chinese language, using other words that sounded or looked similar to replace those sensitive words, such as "freedom" and "democracy."

President Xi Jinping removed the term limit (two 5-year terms) set by Deng Xiaoping by instructing lawmakers to modify the Chinese constitution. That was a move backward to the Mao era of leaders holding office until they died. The Chinese government also cracked down on underground Christian family churches. Most younger generations of Chinese people were so brainwashed that they were very loyal to the Chinese Communist Party. I think it would probably take a long time for China to embark on a democratic path, and that it would be interesting yet disturbing to see if Xi would serve a third term as the top leader of China.

I received a conditional green card because I was married to a U.S. citizen. Two years later, I got my official green card as a permanent resident. Before I went back to China in 2007, I did not apply for a re-entry permit, and my green card became invalid. After I came back in the U.S. in 2010, I had to adjust my immigration status. Through that process, I got my green card again. In 2014, I met the requirements to become a naturalized U.S. citizen. I submitted my application and followed the process. My interview was scheduled for a day in May.

I spent some time to seriously study the civics test study materials, which covered the U.S. political system and history. It started off by teaching about the constitution, such as that nobody is above the law, including the government. This is very different from China. In China, the Chinese Communist Party leads everything. I practiced the test questions, and by the time of the interview date, I was very familiar with those 100 test questions.

The day of the interview was a sunny day. I wore a black short sleeve shirt, a black blazer, and black pants. After I sent the boys to school, D drove me to the train station in New Brunswick. I took the train to Newark and walked to the federal office building.

After going through the security check, I entered the waiting room. The waiting room was full of people from different ethnic backgrounds. I arrived early. I waited a long time, until an officer called my name. The officer was a white male in his fifties. He took me to his office, where I was sworn in. He made photocopies of my Chinese passport and asked me to submit my tax return. He asked me to read an English sentence and asked me to write the answer to that question on a piece of paper to test my ability to read and write English. Then he asked me six questions from the civics test. I answered all of them correctly and passed the test. He asked me, if necessary, would I be willing to defend the United States? I answered yes. He asked me about elections, and I said I would like to exercise my voting rights. The officer congratulated me for passing the interview, asked me to sign some documents, and escorted me out to the waiting room to wait for the naturalization ceremony.

While waiting, I received a small U.S. flag and a big envelope with a welcome letter from President Obama. Soon, it was time for the ceremony. An officer let us listen to a patriotic song and watch a video on immigration. I was moved to tears watching how immigrants from different countries and times came to the U.S. and became U.S. citizens. We sang the national anthem, the "Star Spangled Banner." We read the pledge, pledging our loyalty to the United States of America. I received my naturalization papers and officially became a U.S. citizen.

CHAPTER 21

*A*s my boys got older, it was time for me to look for work. I applied to jobs and got a few interviews, but I did not get any offers. I even went to New York City for some interviews. There was a bus route nearby going to New York City, but it took an hour and a half each way in normal traffic. It was not feasible for me to commute to jobs located there. I got a few freelance market research projects which I worked on from home, but those projects were hard to find and could not produce a steady income. I also tried to take the NCLEX nursing licensure exam, but the credentialing process was too demanding, and I could not get some of the required documents from China. I had quit nursing before China started to have a licensure program. I never got my nursing license in China.

I still did not feel comfortable driving. It took too long for me to decide to turn when I had to make a left turn. I would drive drivers behind me crazy. So, I decided not to drive. Without being able to drive, the kind of jobs I could do were limited.

One day, one of the readers of my blog left me a message telling me I could work as a translator because of my good command in both English and Chinese. I reached out to him asking him how to find those jobs. He told me to sign up at Proz. com, a website connecting translators to customers who needed translation services. I signed up, but I did not get many translation jobs. After one year on this website, I received an email from the recruiting department of one of the largest interpreting companies in the U.S. through the website. It was a legitimate work-from-home job opportunity. I was interested and followed the instructions to apply for the interpreting job. I spoke with the recruiter who taught me some basics of interpreting. I took the exam. A few days later, they notified me that I was accepted.

I started to work from home as a Mandarin interpreter over the phone. I got non-stop calls. I got all kinds of calls - calls from banks, insurance companies, department stores, utility companies, and 911 calls. Calls were monitored by the quality assurance department. I received periodic feedback which helped me to improve.

While I applied to that company, I also applied to a few other companies. I went through their hiring processes and took tests. One of these other companies offered me a higher paying video interpreting job. I gladly accepted and quit my job at the large over-the-phone interpreting company. At the new company, calls were mostly medical calls. Doctors or nurses would place calls on our platform on iPads mounted on stands, calls got routed to our workstations, and we would answer those video calls to interpret for them, to help them communicate with their patients with limited English proficiency.

One day, I got a call. A Chinese woman came in to get an abortion. In the U.S., the delivery of health services follows certain processes, and patients are fully informed along these processes. Even for minor procedures such as abortion, doctors and anesthesiologists would come to speak with the patients about the procedures, their benefits, risks and alternatives. Patients need to sign consent forms based on their understanding of these things. Such processes can take longer than the actual procedure.

On that call, the nurse came to ask about the patient's medical and family history. She also asked about allergies. The anesthesiologist and doctor came in and spoke with the patient. I interpreted faithfully.

After the doctor left, we waited for the nurse to come in to place an IV before the patient went to the operating room. The wait was a little long. The patient spoke with me while we were waiting. She said that the processes were so complicated here. If she were to go to the clinic in Chinatown, it would have only taken a little over 10 minutes, and she would already be out and headed home. She told me she already had two sons. This pregnancy was unplanned. Her husband and mother-in-law did not really want her to abort the baby. I just listened to her politely. As she spoke, she started to hesitate. When the nurse came in, I interpreted to the nurse that the patient was hesitant and changed her mind. The nurse said she needed to report to the doctor.

The doctor came and patiently told the patient her options. The patient was eight weeks pregnant. The doctor told her if she changed her mind again after going home, she could always come back to do the abortion again. She told the patient the baby was healthy. If she wanted, she could carry the baby to term, and that she would have a 50% chance of having a girl. After hearing she could have a girl, the patient was happy and was firmer in keeping the baby. The patient was happy with the doctor and wanted to see her for her prenatal visits.

The story had a happy ending. Because of full communication, a precious life was saved. I was happy to facilitate in the process as an interpreter. I followed the interpreter's code of ethics, remained impartial, and helped the patient to overcome language barriers to have meaningful conversations with her healthcare providers and make a choice that was based on her own wishes. In the U.S., many hospitals or clinics provide free interpretation services to their patients.

That is just one example of what I do on this job. Two years later, I became a full-time employee at this company, through which I purchased health insurance for my entire family. I also contracted with a few other companies to do over-the-phone interpreting work when I was not working on my full-time job.

The company I worked for full-time probably had the best video interpreting technology and platform. It could support high-definition, stable video calls with relatively small bandwidth usage. Video interpreting is closer to on-site interpreting than over-the-phone interpreting but with more flexibility, which was welcomed by our customers. They could call us on-demand, 24/7. Our company had a strong tech support team to maintain and update our platform. When we encountered technical issues, we could ask for help in the tech support channel on Teams or call our tech support team's help line. They would sometimes remote into our computers to help us resolve problems. Our company's business expanded fast. Our Mandarin team multiplied over the course of just a few years.

The biggest benefit of a remote job was being able to work from home. It suited me especially well since I was not confident in driving and had school-aged children at home. It saved commuting time. When I joined, I submitted my preferred hours, and my manager and the scheduler reviewed and then approved them as my set schedule. The hours I chose were mainly hours when the kids were at school, with breaks set up for picking them up after school was over. Although my hours were mostly peak hours with lots of calls, I got to take care of and spend time with my kids. Our hours of work also had some flexibility. Whenever something happened so that we needed to take time off, or when we wanted to go on vacation, we could apply for paid time off following company procedure. We could also swap shifts with our teammates. If we ever needed to move, I could relocate my workstation to any state in the U.S.

Unlike other remote interpreting companies, this company had a great culture of teamwork. Although we worked remotely, we used Microsoft Teams software to stay connected with co-workers and the management teams. We had Teams channels, which we used to share terminology, knowledge of certain illnesses, and interesting cases (of course omitting any personally identifiable information and protected health information according to HIPAA laws). Our manager also created a "Watercooler" channel for us to share jokes or interesting non-job-related topics. We had a pair of funny twin brothers and a number of other teammates who posted jokes daily in the Watercooler channel. Inspired by a teammate from Taiwan who was good at writing Tang Dynasty (618 to 907 A.D.) style poems ("Tang Shi"), I also started to write them. (I will attach some of these poems at the end of my memoir for people who can read Chinese to enjoy.) During some parts of the 2020 Covid-19 pandemic, our call volume reduced. When we were not on calls, we frequented the Watercooler channel and had lots of fun. For a while, the "Watercooler" was flooded with toilet tissue shortage memes.

We could also have direct, private chats with our colleagues and managers. Sometimes we also had video meetings with our managers. I met a teammate who lived in neighboring Pennsylvania in person a few times. I also made some other good friends among my teammates even without ever meeting any of them. Based on my teammates' chats in the Teams channels, I could tell their personalities. Since I only answered phone calls at other over-the-phone interpreting companies I contracted with previously, I didn't have such interactions with my coworkers at these other companies.

As I mentioned earlier, my job was helping patients who spoke Mandarin but had low English proficiency to cross language barriers to communicate effectively with English-speaking healthcare providers. Among those people who needed our help were visitors, patients or immigrants from Mainland China, often the elderly. There were also people from Taiwan, Hong Kong, and other countries or areas. Using qualified medical interpreters is better than using family or friends for accuracy and neutrality. All of our interpreters had passed rigorous tests and were qualified medical interpreters. We had to adhere to the high ethical standards of the interpreting industry. Some of our colleagues were nationally certified. I also received my national medical interpreting certificate after passing both written and oral tests, making me a CMI in Mandarin from the NBCMI, National Board of Certification for Medical Interpreters.

Most of our calls were regular doctor visits, ER visits, specialist visits, or calls related to surgical consent, discharge instructions, and so on. We also had labor and deliver sessions that could last quite long. After interpreting "Take a deep breath, hold, push" for a long time, when a baby was finally born, we felt very happy. Sometimes we also had to tell bad news to patients or their families, such as announcing the diagnosis of terminal illnesses, death, or discussing hospice care. These could be hard.

This job required concentration; however, after we logged out, we didn't have to worry about anything anymore - no more stress. One other benefit of working as a medical interpreter was that we got to see all kinds of cases. We learned medical knowledge and how the U.S. healthcare system worked.

The biggest language my company serviced was Spanish. Mandarin and Cantonese were two of our high-demand languages. We had a dedicated Cantonese team. Our Mandarin and Cantonese interpreters shared the same Microsoft Teams channels. We were one big team. The diversity of the United States drove the growth of our business. I was very happy to grow with the company, to witness our success. I loved my remote interpreting job.

Our business was not as hard hit as some other businesses during the 2020 Covid-19 pandemic. I had a job throughout the pandemic while millions of people lost their jobs. My job was fully remote. Working from home allowed me to minimize risk of exposure to the deadly virus. I was one of the lucky ones.

CHAPTER 22

$\mathcal{S}$ ince my last episode of bipolar disorder relapse while we were in China, I had been taking medicine under the care of my primary care doctor in northern New Jersey. After we moved to South Brunswick in central New Jersey, I started to see a psychiatrist on regular basis to manage my mental illness as recommended by my new primary care doctor. Upon my request, the psychiatrist changed my medicine to a weight-neutral, atypical anti-psychotic medicine.

While I was on this medicine, I did not sleep very well. I still had episodes of impulsive shopping. I bought things I did not need online. Then I became depressed. A few things might have triggered it. I was worried about my younger son S's attention deficit disorder. I had just had a meeting with the school about it. I was also working on a tedious translation project from a translation agency in New York City. It was a simple project - translating 300 Chinese IDs issued by the Chinese government. It was very simple, but tedious. I had to be very careful not to enter the numbers wrong. That was not one of my strengths. I over-estimated my output, and it turned out to be impossible to complete the task by the deadline. I was stressed.

I began to be sensitive to D's behavior. I became sentimental. I would cry over minor things that made me upset. I developed insomnia and a headache. My depression was like a pair of colored glasses distorting my perception of the world around me. I noticed more of the negative sides of things and enlarged them.

I started to have suicidal thoughts. I felt it was too painful to continue to live. Dying would be a relief – that was how I truly felt then. For the sake of my young children, I would not take any actions to end my life. However, those suicidal thoughts kept lingering in my mind. I did not lose full control, so I searched for a suicide prevention hotline and made a phone call to seek help. I spoke to a trained volunteer, telling her I had trouble communicating with my husband. I cried as I spoke. The volunteer listened to me quietly and gave me a few supportive words here and there. It felt good to talk to someone.

My husband noticed my abnormal behavior. He told me to call my psychiatrist. I also realized I needed help from my doctor. I got an appointment for the next day, and D drove me to see the doctor. The doctor adjusted my medication and added another medicine that could help me with my sleep and depression.

I took those medicines as directed by my psychiatrist after I came home. After about 10 days, my condition improved. I got out of that episode of depression with the help of medicine.

Life went on as usual, still pretty much the same without any big changes. It still had the same imperfections, but it did not bother me anymore, and I could handle those imperfections again.

Depression and bipolar disorder are treatable illnesses. They are caused by imbalances of brain chemistry. Modern medicines can restore those balances. Symptoms go away once those balances were restored. After walking out of depression, we should accept our imperfections and the world around us. We can put things into perspective and no longer enlarge the negative side of things.

In order to not mislead my readers, I do not mention the names of the medicine I took or am taking on purpose. Everyone's condition is different. It is important to talk to your own doctor about what medicine is the best for you if you have similar illnesses.

I have met people who see doctors but do not take their medicine as prescribed. They worry too much about the side effects. Doctors are well-trained professionals with ample experience in their field. Medicines on the market also have gone through rigorous testing and clinical trials. After launch, they are still under market surveillance. If serious side effects are reported and investigated, any unsafe medicine would be pulled off the market to ensure patient safety.

When we go to see doctors, we form a trusting relationship with them. To treat illnesses, patients need to comply with their doctor's treatment plan, including taking medicine and making lifestyle changes, the latter of which can be more difficult to achieve. Taking medicine often is easier. I have seen way too many people who would rather listen to their friends' hearsay than believe in their well-trained and experienced healthcare professionals.

My sister once told me she had a friend in his 40s with high blood pressure, and that she had met him at a gathering recently and spoken with him. He had told her his blood pressure was very high, with systolic blood pressure running 160 to 170. My sister had asked him if he took blood pressure medicine. He had said he did not take blood pressure medicine for fear of side effects. Not long after that gathering, my sister heard he had bleeding in his brainstem and fell into a vegetative state. He probably has died by now. If he had taken his medicine, his blood pressure would have been under control, and he might still have been living. The side effects would most likely be well-tolerated.

I also took medicine to manage my type 2 diabetes. With daily insulin injections and some oral diabetes medicine, my diabetes had always been under good control. I had not developed any diabetic complications so far after been diagnosed with type 2 diabetes over ten years earlier. I spoke with the painter in his mid-30s who helped to paint the walls of my home office. He told me he had type 1 diabetes. He had an insulin pump, his glucose was under good control, and he could live a normal life and enjoy a high quality of life. Modern medicines work wonders in treating many once-deadly illnesses.

When it comes to mental health medication, patients tend to have poor compliance. Many of these patients think that they just have some stress in life, that they are not ill and do not need to take medicine which comes with side effects. If doctors prescribe medicine, patients should trust the doctors' professional judgement and take the medicine to get better. It is important to also make changes to one's lifestyle or cognitive patterns, but taking medicine as prescribed is the first step to recovery. At this point, it would also be helpful to see a behavioral therapist to help with making cognitive changes. After taking medicine, if one feels discomfort due to side effects, he or she could talk to the doctor to make adjustments. It is also important to allow some time for mental health medication to take effect.

Eight months after I recovered from my short depressive episode, the 2016 election was approaching its defining moments. I supported Hillary Clinton. I thought she was very competent with an outstanding resume. I hoped she could make history by becoming the first female president of the United States of America. It was time for a woman to shatter the glass ceiling and hold the country's highest office. I watched CNN. I listened to her speeches. I also made donations to her campaign.

I joined a few Chinese groups on the popular Chinese social media app WeChat. People in these groups were mostly strangers, and they were interested in debating about the election. Soon, I encountered hostility in some of the right-wing groups. Whenever I posted anything supporting democratic values, I got nasty attacks. I became too involved, and those attacks affected me in a negative way. I became agitated, and I could not slow down my thoughts. I lost sleep. I was also taking a medicine that is not very strong in preventing bipolar relapses. By the time I reached out to my psychiatrist, it was too late. I had a bad relapse on election day. I did not get to cast my vote. It would have been the first presidential election vote I ever casted in my whole life.

I became totally incoherent. D had to call 911 to take me to the ER. I lost my memory. I could not remember what happened at the hospital. I was later transferred to two other hospitals and ended up at a mental hospital at the southern end of central New Jersey. This was my third stay at a mental hospital and my first time staying at a U.S. mental hospital. I don't know why those hospitals did not contact my psychiatrist. The medicine they gave me did not work. I stayed at the hospital over Thanksgiving holiday, of which I had no recollection.

It was close to Christmas when they finally put me back on the atypical antipsychotic medicine that had always worked before to get my illness under control. I started to regain my coherence. The mental hospital was very busy during the holiday season. It was understaffed. Many new patients were hospitalized. Some were agitated, cursing the staff tirelessly. One female patient told me she was very rich and gave me her address on a piece of paper (which I turned in to the staff following the hospital guidelines). As I got better, I could not sleep at the hospital. At night, the lights in the hallway were very bright and shone into my room. Every 15 minutes a staff member would shine a light on me and other patients to prevent suicide. He or she would document his or her observations in a big binder, and as he or she turned the page, it would make a loud noise. It was impossible for me to sleep. After I was discharged and went home, it took me months to restore my sleep, with the help of sleeping pills on top of my psychiatric medicine.

As I got better, I was asked to join therapy groups. Those were meaningless for me. I had trouble following the therapists. I started to call my husband. He took family leave from his work to take care of the boys. With me gone for so long it was very difficult for him and the boys, who were 9 and 10 years old at that time. He came to visit me a few times. My Baha'i friend and neighbor T also came to visit me a few times and brought me lotions and other personal care products allowed by the hospital. I had panic attacks during the day and was given anxiety medicine.

I wanted to leave the hospital to go home. The doctor in charge wanted to keep me at the hospital for longer. From one of the other doctors, I learned that I could request to go to court to present my case to a judge, who would then decide if I could go home. I told the social worker I wanted to go to the court. The court was held on Fridays at the mental hospital. D came on the court day. After listening to my case, the judge decided that I could go home. I was finally discharged on a rainy day in early January, after being hospitalized for more than 50 days.

After I was discharged, the hospital arranged for me to attend one and a half months of group therapy at an outpatient behavioral health center. I met a psychiatrist there who recommended another newer medicine to me. Once again, I did not find the group therapies very helpful for me. After completion of the group therapy, I followed up with my previous psychiatrist. I asked him about the newer medicine the psychiatrist at the behavioral health center recommended. My psychiatrist said it was a very effective medicine and was weight-neutral. He switched me to this medicine, and I have been taking it since. It was indeed a very good medicine. I felt hardly any side effects.

D's company did not honor his right to take family leave to care for a sick family member and terminated his employment after I was discharged. It was a very difficult time. I still could not work, and D became unemployed. I reached out to my friends. Many of my friends offered kind help by sending us checks. My business school classmates donated around $20,000 and sent the money to me through my sister in several installments. This outpouring of support helped us to live through a very difficult time in my life.

CHAPTER 23

Later, I resumed my work at the video remote interpreting company. I worked reduced hours at first, and later on I resumed my previous working hours as I got better. D continued to be unemployed except for a short contract job. D did not want to move to any other cities that he could not commute . He wanted the boys to stay at their schools with their friends. Local jobs were harder to find for him. I worked close to 70 hours every week between two jobs - the full-time video remote interpreting job, which offered healthcare benefits for the whole family, and a part-time contract over-the-phone interpreting job with several companies. I changed my schedule at my full-time job so that I could fit in two jobs. I was able to make enough money to support our family of four. It was long hours, but I would take a 15-minute break every few hours. I would lie down to rest my back, and it helped.

After D lost his job and before I became a full-time employee at the video remote interpreting company and got healthcare coverage for our family, we enrolled in Obamacare insurance through the health insurance marketplace. No matter how some people criticized Obamacare, it helped many people like us to get healthcare coverage.

While I worked long hours, D did grocery shopping, laundry, cleaning, cooking and other chores. He was very handy. He did repairs around the house. Our old oven broke down, and after we purchased a new oven on Amazon, D did the installation all by himself. He also put a lot of effort into cooking and kept coming up with new ideas for food that would be interesting for me and the boys. While the boys were doing remote learning during the Covid-19 pandemic (in middle school, in the seventh and eighth grades now), D followed up with them to make sure they were on track with their studies and assignments. D and I made a good team to live through a difficult time.

My sister brought her family to visit us in January 2019. It was not easy for them to get a visa to come to the U.S. to visit us. They had to go to the U.S. consulate in Shanghai to go through interviews with immigration officers. I wrote them a good invitation letter following examples I found online. Luckily, they passed their interviews. My brother-in-law, my sister, and their daughter R arrived in the U.S. to see us. D did not want to go to the airport in Newark to pick them up. They took an Uber to get to our home. I was very happy to see them. I had not seen them in almost nine years. R had grown into a beautiful teenager. My sister told me Taoma had become a Christian. After raising her granddaughter, the daughter of her youngest son, she continued to work in the city of Wuhu as a caregiver.

It was their first time visiting the U.S. They could only stay for about 10 days. I booked two short tours through a travel agency run by Chinese people. They visited Niagara Falls, Philadelphia, and Washington D.C. on those tours. I took time off and took them to tour New York city. It was very cold on those days. They stayed at our house when they were not on those tours. They walked around our neighborhood and liked our environment. I also took them to an outlet mall to shop for name-brand clothes that were sold at very high prices in China. It was a lot cheaper to buy them here in the U.S. We treated them to American food such as turkey and corned beef and cabbage. R brought her homework on the trip and had to do homework everyday while she was here. She was a high-schooler and would soon take the college entrance exam. Soon, they left. My sister said she would come to visit us again after her daughter went to college. As a U.S. citizen, I could sponsor my sister's immigration to the U.S., although they would have had to wait for a long time through a lengthy process. I asked her about this, but she declined. She was happy with her life in China.

My father-in-law passed away in 2019 peacefully surrounded by his three children. D did not get to go to California to attend his funeral. D was sad for days. Later on, my sister-in-law sent D many items from his late father. D cherished them.

During the 2020 presidential election, I did not follow the news and did not join any political groups on WeChat or Facebook. (I left those hostile groups after I got ill in 2016.) I received my mail-in ballot and voted by mail early. I cast my

first presidential election vote in my life based on my values
there were no true elections in China, so I never voted while
I was there. I support stricter gun control, gay marriage, and
women's rights to have access to safe abortions. I also support
the development and use of renewable energy to curb global
warming to save our planet.

Joe Biden won the election. However, Trump would not
accept the fact that he lost and concede. He said the very same
voting system which elected him to office in 2016 was rigged
in 2020. A lot of his supporters believed in his claims of wide-
spread voter fraud which they could not even prove. Politics is so
divisive in the U.S. I hope my friends and readers with different
ideas will respect mine as I respect theirs. I hope we can still be
friends. I hope that on January 20 the new president elect will
take office smoothly and turn a new page in U.S. history.

We are lucky to live in a democratic country. We elect our
government officials. The country is not ruled by just one party
like the Chinese Communist Party that controlled everything.
We the people have the right to choose through voting. If our
officials do not do their jobs well, we the people vote them out
of office. We should protect the democratic system that has been
in existence in this great country for over 200 years.

I hope D will be able to find work after the pandemic is
over. With vaccines available, I hope the pandemic will soon be
over. Regardless, I will continue to work hard to support our
family. I have been taking the newer weight-neutral antipsychotic

medicine. I see my psychiatrist every other month, or sooner if needed. Whenever I feel any symptoms such as poor sleep or racing thoughts, I call my psychiatrist to adjust my medication. It's been over four years since my last episode of bipolar relapse. I have been very careful with taking my medicine every single day. I hope I will have no more relapses. I hope I will be able to continue working until retirement age.

Bipolar disorder cannot be cured at this moment. However, there are effective medicines to manage it, to get it under control. Like I wrote earlier, every patient's condition is different. It is important to find a psychiatrist that one can trust and to take their medicine as prescribed. My medicines balance my brain chemicals so that I can think and behave normally and live a normal life. It does not affect my intelligence or other functions. I am smart and creative. I am a loving, strong, and hard-working person. I am a good wife, a good mother, a good friend, and a good worker. I am not ashamed of having bipolar disorder. It is just one of the many illnesses people can get. It is just one of the challenges I have in my life.

I am grateful to my husband, my children, my sister, my father, my parents-in-law and other in-laws, my friends, and my coworkers. As said by one of my former managers, I am a resilient person. Every time I have been struck down by difficulties, I have risen up strong.

With all those challenges, I am still a lucky person. I got what I wanted most in my life - a family of my own. I am blessed.

I left the country I was born in. I flew over the Pacific Ocean and became a U.S. citizen for life, liberty, and the pursuit of happiness. I love my new country. I will spend the rest of my life in the U.S. I hope my children will grow up safely and live happy lives in this country.

I hope my humble story will inspire people with similar challenges. Thank you for reading my memoir.

P.S. My father passed away in February 2021 at the age of 87 shortly after he fell sick. I miss him and he will live in my heart forever.

APPENDIX

My Tang-Style Poems in Simplified Chinese

咏春

桃花点点红, 春韵日渐浓。

冬去影无踪, 可把棉衣送。

当年在江东, 风景大不同。

宅家心意空, 乡思如泉涌。

思亲

春梦偶伤悲, 醒来尤带泪。

老父及小妹, 依然在关内。

一别十年飞, 不得再相会。

路遥盘缠贵, 何日省亲归。

赞吾儿

两个小儿郎, 年龄皆相仿。

上学为同窗, 结伴读书忙。

天真写脸庞, 笑容很俊朗。

性格不鲁莽, 前途正宽广。

时光

时光飞逝太匆忙,转瞬小儿成俊郎。

童颜留在照片上,温馨回忆驻心房。

岁月

岁月催人老,无有长生药。

来日日益少,每天要过好。

莫要太操劳,健康是个宝。

避免寻烦恼,经常开口笑。

姻缘

新姻缘易覆辙蹈,不如将就过到老。

磕磕绊绊架常吵,一般也没大烦恼。

平凡夫妻是对宝,人生相伴莫可少。

待到孙辈膝下绕,晚年回忆无限好。

春思

清晨起薄雾,花开微带露。

柳条随风舞,春光惹人慕。

异乡把日度,思亲亦如故。

此情同今古,赋诗来相诉。

自嘲

年过半百鬓发花,已然为母育两娃。

远嫁胡人听胡笳,梦里不知在天涯。

赏春

群芳沐煦风，峰飞花丛中。

授粉正匆匆，争相把蕊宠。

赏春意兴浓，休闲享轻松。

怀想众亲朋，他年再相逢。

春景图

鸟鸣声声脆，春光惹人醉。

旭日放光辉，风景真明媚。

寒意已消退，遍野开花卉。

层林尽染翠，山川如画绘。

咏腊梅

门前腊梅花，芳馨沁我家。

严寒不惧怕，隆冬绽奇葩。

剪枝瓶中插，摆放东窗下。

暗香阵阵发，思乡不能罢。

牡丹

牡丹傲群芳，贵为花中王。

沐浴好春光，一朵独绽放。

主人思故乡，此物可疗伤。

种植院中央，且与路人赏。

鸢尾花

艳丽鸢尾花，傲立红墙下。
茎叶很挺拔，绘入梵高画。

越洋女

有个小姑娘，曾住长江旁。
皖南是家乡，度过好时光。
长大越重洋，远隔天一方。
暮色渐苍茫，终老在异邦。

大雪

大雪压枝头，老公直犯愁。
积雪两尺厚，铲雪累成猴。

西游记-唐僧

大唐有高僧，礼佛伴青灯。
奉旨来应征，西方去朝圣。
路险禽兽猛，妖魔面目狰。
耗尽他毕生，真经终取成。

西游记-孙悟空

金猴生顽石，上天闹瑶池。
受罚千年逝，玄奘把恩施。
欣然来拜师，朝夕勤服侍。
妖魔百般试，故事传万世。

西游记-猪八戒

天蓬元帅凡间坠，高老庄上欲入赘。

棒打鸳鸯美梦碎，西天取经路途累。

西游记-白骨精

千年白骨精，修炼成妖灵。

骷髅化人形，貌美步轻盈。

出没荒山岭，时有露狰狞。

且把唐僧迎，不教取真经。

天仙配

仙女下凡天仙配，牛郎织女来相会。

你耕田来我主炊，织布做衣缝棉被。

养儿育女过年岁，人间日月无限美。

天庭难容欲怪罪，王母拔簪银河绘。

两岸对面把泪垂，化作恒星夜空缀。

七夕鹊桥聚一回，千古爱情终不悔。

白蛇传

白蛇报恩嫁许仙

法海凶狠将怒迁

斗法大水漫金山

雷峰塔压数百年

阿娇

吾家有女叫阿娇,如花似玉有细腰。
搔首弄姿媚眼抛,招蜂引蝶太风骚。
七媒八聘上花轿,鸳鸯帐里把魂销。
恩爱缠绵度春宵,芳华永驻老来俏。

青楼女子

卖身入青楼,且把琵琶搂。
周旋于人流,颜色难长久。
热闹终将休,情郎再难候。
年老添忧愁,谁人怜惜否。

财赋

努力挣钱不嫌苦,入夜欢喜把钱数。
遇难莫打退堂鼓,坚持撒网将财捕。
购置良田千百亩,万贯修造黄金府。
红颜仕女抱琴抚,逍遥自在温泉谷。

行乐歌

行乐须及时,举杯不宜迟。
过村此店逝,速把佳酿试。
当垆俏娘子,机敏赛卓氏。
且从相如师,谱写罗曼史。

肥

羡慕唐朝杨贵妃, 体态丰腴是为美。
不必节食来减肥, 瘦得前胸贴后背。
吃吃喝喝享美味, 开开心心把觉睡。
心宽体胖终无悔, 坚决不做饿死鬼。

白发添

脑满肠肥大肚腩, 吟诗作对乐无边。
辗转反侧夜难眠, 绞尽脑汁白发添。

美女

遥看一美女, 想娶做伴侣。
不料天下雨, 厚妆难以续。
弃之如弊履, 人间悲喜剧。
貌美其实虚, 莫如心相许。

老顽童

调皮捣蛋老顽童, 翻译公司粉丝众。
爱开玩笑人来疯, 逗得大家捧腹痛。

看牙

无齿大妈缺牙巴, 高明牙医乐开花。
种植牙齿好吃瓜, 牙医钞票大把抓。
大妈直把牙医夸, 牙医听了笑哈哈。
能吃鱼来能吃虾, 大妈满意传佳话。

镜湖泛舟

夏夜泛舟镜湖上，青春激扬放歌唱。
纯洁友谊涓流长，美好记忆永难忘。

秋怨（借王维诗"山居秋暝"的韵脚）

夕阳西下后，天凉好个秋。
皓月透窗照，对镜把泪流。
深闺寂寞女，思慕泛轻舟。
夜阑人俱歇，青春不可留。

玲珑心

七巧玲珑心，几人能赏欣。
寂寞到如今，独自把诗吟。
离别故人亲，万里隔洋津。
近处无芳邻，空等座上宾。

游子心

日落黄昏近，倦鸟已归林。
夜幕正降临，衾冷难就寝。
思亲泪沾巾，寂寞游子心。
红烛快燃尽，异乡度光阴。

半梦半醒

在半梦半醒时分, 脸上竟挂着泪痕。

夜深尚未到清晨, 摸索起身点青灯。

一片寂静刚三更, 独眠衾寒周身冷。

盼望晨曦促星沉, 又迎一天悄开门。

家在心安处

学诗且仿古, 常诉思乡苦。

谢君来慰抚, 吾深受鼓舞。

入乡即随俗, 可把风物读。

小屋春风沐, 家在心安处。

樱桃

初夏正晴好, 樱桃成熟了。

吾儿采摘下, 慈母炉中烤。

黑莓

盛夏绿正肥

院中采黑莓

做成甜点美

幸福满心扉

酒酿元宵

来碗酒酿元宵
一盘爆炒猪腰
喝茶来把酒消
一同共度良宵

赏蟹

秋风扬
蟹脚痒
把酒烫
美味享
旧时光
梦里想
太难忘
浊泪淌